13 STEPS TO BLOODY GOOD MARKS

ASHWIN SANGHI
ASHOK RAJANI

First published by Westland Publications Private Limited in 2017

Published by Westland Books, a division of Nasadiya Technologies
Private Limited in 2023

No. 269/2B, First Floor, 'Irai Arul', Vimalraj Street, Nethaji Nagar, Alapakkam
Main Road, Maduravoyal, Chennai 600095

Westland and the Westland logo are the trademarks of Nasadiya Technologies
Private Limited, or its affiliates.

Copyright © Ashwin Sanghi, 2017

Ashwin Sanghi asserts the moral right to be identified as the author of
this work.

ISBN: 9789395767804

10 9 8 7 6 5 4 3 2 1

The views and opinions expressed in this work are the author's own and the facts
are as reported by him, and the publisher is in no way liable for the same.

All rights reserved

Typeset by SŪRYA, New Delhi

Printed at Nutech Print Services-India

No part of this book may be reproduced, or stored in a retrieval system, or
transmitted in any form or by any means, electronic, mechanical, photocopying,
recording, or otherwise, without express written permission of the publisher.

13 STEPS TO BLOODY GOOD MARKS

Ashwin Sanghi is counted among India's highest selling English authors. He has written several bestsellers (*The Rozabal Line, Chanakya's Chant, The Krishna Key, The Sialkot Saga, Keepers of the Kalachakra, The Vault of Vishnu,* and *The Magicians of Mazda* in his *Bharat Series*) and two *New York Times* bestselling crime thrillers with James Patterson, *Private India* (sold in the US as *City on Fire*) and *Private Delhi* (sold in the US as *Count to Ten*). Ashwin also mentors, co-writes and edits titles in this popular *13 Steps Series* on subjects as diverse as Luck, Wealth, Marks, Health and Parenting.

He is a regular contributor to the Op-Ed pages of the *Times of India*. Ashwin has been included by *Forbes India* in their Celebrity 100 and by the *New Indian Express* in their Culture Power List. He is a winner of the Crossword Popular Choice Award 2012, Atta Galatta Popular Choice Award 2018, WBR Iconic Achievers Award 2018, the Lit-O-Fest Literature Legend Award 2018, the Kalinga Popular Choice Award 2021 and the Deendayal Upadhyaya Recognition 2023. He was educated at Cathedral and John Connon School, Mumbai, and St Xavier's College, Mumbai. He holds a Master's from Yale University, USA, and a D. Litt. (Honoris Causa) from JECRC University, Rajasthan. Ashwin lives in Mumbai with his wife, Anushika, and his son, Raghuvir.

Website: www.sanghi.in
Facebook: www.facebook.com/ashwinsanghi
Twitter: www.twitter.com/ashwinsanghi
YouTube: www.youtube.com/ashwinsanghi
Instagram: instagram.com/ashwin.sanghi

Ashok L. Rajani was educated in St. Mary's High School, Chennai, Loyola College, Chennai, and College of Engineering, Guindy. He joined Andhra Bank as a departmental officer in 1978, took the banking exam (CAIIB), completed an MBA (Finance) and went on to teach in the bank's Staff Training College. After retiring, he taught himself the APA guidelines and edited engineering-related technical papers and Ph.D. theses of Indian and international candidates. He also taught freelance classes on communication skills and management for B.B.A. and M.B.A. students while editing several books for Indian, British and American authors.

Ashok speaks five languages and resides in Chennai with his wife, Sulochana, who is a gynaecologist. He has a son, Siddarth and two grandchildren. Teaching is his first love.

You can connect with Ashok via the following channels:

Facebook: www.facebook.com/Ashok Lr
LinkedIn: http://in.linkedin.com/in/ashok-lr-20769210

CONTENTS

FOREWORD	*vii*
INTRODUCTION	*ix*
STEP 1: BUS—(B)ELIEVE, (U)NLEARN AND WORK (S)MART	*1*
STEP 2: FAIL TO PLAN = PLAN TO FAIL	*9*
STEP 3: MAKE CLASSES COUNT	*21*
STEP 4: BE CONSISTENT AFTER CLASS	*34*
STEP 5: MASTER THE SCIENCE OF READING	*49*
STEP 6: BOOST YOUR MEMORY QUOTIENT	*61*
STEP 7: PRACTICE MAKES PERFECT	*84*
STEP 8: BUILD YOUR NETWORK	*95*
STEP 9: SHARPEN SUPPLEMENTARY SKILLS	*104*
STEP 10: MANAGE YOUR ENVIRONMENT	*114*

STEP 11: MANAGE BODY AND MIND	*120*
STEP 12: EXAM STRATEGY	*131*
STEP 13: GOING BEYOND MARKS	*140*
THE FOURTEENTH	*143*
REFERENCES	*146*

FOREWORD

After I wrote *13 Steps to Bloody Good Luck* in 2014, I received many messages from readers saying that the book had helped them in gaining a new perspective regarding their lives. This led to a second book in the series, *13 Steps to Bloody Good Wealth*, for which I collaborated with Sunil Dalal, someone who truly has a unique perspective on wealth creation.

Among the messages that I received after the book on luck was one from a student. She wondered whether a book along the *13 Steps* pattern could be developed to help students like her study better and thus score better marks. I instantly thought of the person who could write it—Ashok Rajani.

Many years ago, when I had released a book in my *Bharat Series* called *The Krishna Key*, I received a rather long email from a stranger. That stranger pointed out some mistakes that I had committed in terms of logic, research and grammar. This was in spite of three rounds of editing. I immediately contacted him and asked him to fact-check my next book. That stranger was Ashok

Rajani. In fact, he went on to become the editor for *13 Steps to Bloody Good Luck*.

Ashok has dabbled in many jobs and all of them have involved an element of teaching. During his school days, he taught his nephews and nieces, then participated in group studies while studying for his B.E. He then taught his own son, held lectures in computerization for bank personnel at the Staff Training College, helped colleagues with their banking exams, held classes on various subjects for B.B.A. and M.B.A. students, assisted Ph.D. scholars with their theses, taught his grandchildren … the list is endless.

I believe that his diverse and rich experience gives him a far more rounded insight into the topic of studying, learning and scoring than, say, a college professor or a coaching class tutor. Specialists tend to have a narrow vision whereas I wanted us to present a book that was far wider in scope. I think we have succeeded in doing precisely that.

It is said that you don't have to be great to start, but you have to start to be great. So, what are you waiting for? Please start!

Ashwin Sanghi
Mumbai, 2017

INTRODUCTION

When Ashwin Sanghi (whom I had never met in person but had only communicated with while editing his *13 Steps to Bloody Good Luck*) invited me to co-author *13 Steps to Bloody Good Marks*, I jumped at the offer. His invitation brought back memories of my many interactions with my class fellows and students (because I learnt a lot while teaching). Over the years, I have been asked questions and have heard innumerable comments, both from students and parents. Some much-repeated, contradictory and strange questions and comments included:

1. Why is it necessary to learn this at all?
2. How can we remember such complicated material?
3. Each teacher teaches only one subject. We students are expected to learn several subjects. That's unfair.
4. Why should we do maths when we have calculators and computers that can do it for us?
5. A passing grade is enough for children in our family. Don't overburden my child.
6. I have performed a *pooja* yesterday at the temple. My child is sure to get good marks.

7. I want to be an athlete. So why should I study? I have the advantage of a sports quota.
8. I plan to be a painter. Why are you making me struggle with science subjects?
9. If I become an engineer, why would I need history, geography, English or other languages?
10. I knew this but forgot it. How do you manage to remember so much?

I have saved the best question for last. It's a question for which I actually did not have any reply: Do you have any shortcut to getting great marks without any effort or without having to spend time studying?

Having never been a full-time teacher or a B.Ed., I threw the last question at well-qualified and experienced teachers known to me. They invariably laughed, thinking that I was either joking, crazy—or both. When they realized that the question had been asked in all seriousness, they provided assorted replies that included:

1. Are you joking? If there is indeed a shortcut, then why are we here?
2. You study hard and you get good marks. It's that simple. QED.
3. If you concentrate in class, you need not study. The lesson gets recorded in your mind.
4. Come back from class, revise your lesson. Prepare for tomorrow's lesson today.
5. Change your diet. Get adequate sleep.

6. Other tuition and coaching classes are useless. Come to me for special coaching. I only charge …
7. Write in a bigger font and fill up as many sheets as you can in your exam paper. Examiners want more, not less.
8. Don't get distracted. We never had distractions like TV, mobile or the Internet. They should be banned. Co-ed schools and colleges too.
9. There's a special *mantra* that you should recite. Want to hear it?
10. Have you tried hypnosis?

Realizing that I was nowhere closer to an answer, I figured that I should begin analyzing the study patterns of students to find out if there was a simpler or more efficient way of studying. My personal experience and intermittent interactions with students over fifty years would also come in handy.

One of my first findings was that study patterns varied widely across curricula. For example, preparation for the Civil Services Exam is very different from preparation for the IIT-JEE and that, in turn, is very different from the pattern of studying for the CBSE Class 10 or the CAT. At one point, I even began to feel that there was simply no way that I could distil the requirements for these different exams into a single and uniform approach. I wasn't sure if a 'one size fits all' approach would work.

So while I did my research and developed a plan, I gave up on the idea of ever presenting this material to anyone. That's when Ashwin Sanghi came along. He thought that it would be possible to come up with common principles of effective studying and learning, irrespective of the type of exam or curriculum. His enthusiasm and confidence convinced me that I could do it. So while I took up Ashwin's challenge, I only overcame my procrastination in stages.

Writing one's first book is truly a unique experience. In the past, I have been sarcastic as a teacher, abrasive as an editor, vitriolic as a reviewer, and ruthless as an examiner. But writing this book has made me appreciate the value of the written word like never before. After a long and complicated labour punctuated by many delays, this book is now finally ready.

The poet Maya Angelou is known to have said, 'Nothing will work unless you do.' I sincerely hope that this book helps thousands of aspiring students to work better and score even better. That is my most sincere wish for each one of you.

Ashok Rajani
Chennai, 2017

STEP 1: BUS—(B)ELIEVE, (U)NLEARN AND WORK (S)MART

The starting point is what I call BUS. As you would have realized, there are three elements to this:

1. Belief: believing in yourself.
2. Unlearn: unlearning old and redundant ways.
3. Smart: learning to work smart instead of simply working hard.

Belief

The twenty-sixth President of the United States, Theodore Roosevelt, once said, 'Believe you can and you're halfway there.' This is absolutely vital. You need to believe that you *can* actually make it happen.

It is said that a young man visited the Greek philosopher, Socrates, in search of wisdom. He was surprised when Socrates took him to a lake and dunked his head under water. As the man struggled to come up for air, Socrates continued holding him under.

Later, after recovering, when the young man asked Socrates why he had nearly drowned him, Socrates replied, 'What was it that you most wanted when you were under water?'

'Air,' the young man replied.

Socrates responded, 'When your desire for wisdom is as great as your desire to breathe, you will find wisdom.'

The fact that you're reading this book tells me that you *do* want to study better and that you *do* want to get better marks. But please remember that this book is a road map, not a magic bullet. So you need to travel the path to reach your destination and actually work towards getting consistently better marks.

It is often joked that the biggest room in the world is the room for improvement. Why not look at this book as that room?

Trust me, you have *everything* that is required to become an ace student. Do you think otherwise? Have you heard of someone called Srikanth Bolla?

Srikanth was born without eyes in a village in Andhra Pradesh. The neighbours advised his parents to smother out the life in him. His uneducated parents, who earned Rs. 20,000 a year, did not heed the misguided advice they received and chose to raise him with love and affection.

Born blind and poor, Srikanth was given the back bench in his village school and not allowed to play with the other kids. His father managed to have him shifted to a school for special children in Hyderabad. Here, he not only learnt to play chess and cricket but excelled in them. He topped his class, even getting an opportunity to work with the late President, Dr. A. P. J. Abdul Kalam in his Lead India project.

He cleared his tenth grade exams (the SSLC) scoring above 90 per cent marks overall. Unfortunately, he was denied the option of entering the science stream because of his disability. Srikanth decided to fight for it legally, finally getting a government order permitting him to opt for science subjects but at 'his own risk'. He even managed to get all his textbooks converted to audio books! He worked exceptionally hard, securing 98 per cent in the twelfth standard board exams.

IIT, BITS and other leading Indian engineering institutions did not permit him to write their entrance exam since he was blind. So Srikanth, then aged 18, became the first international blind student to be admitted to the prestigious Massachusetts Institute of Technology (MIT) in the US.

After finishing his studies at MIT, he decided to give up the opportunity that corporate America offered and returned to India in search of creative solutions to generate employment. Today, Srikanth is an entrepreneur with four production plants that manufacture eco-friendly, disposable consumer packaging solutions. A fifth plant, entirely solar power operated, is coming up in Andhra

Pradesh. He has a workforce comprising 70 per cent people with disabilities and a sales turnover of Rs. 500 million.

Srikanth reiterates his conviction: 'If the world looks at me and says, "Srikanth, you can do nothing," I look back at the world and say, "I can do anything."'

Napoleon Hill, the author of *Think and Grow Rich*, said, 'Whatever the mind of man can conceive and believe, it can achieve.' This is what I need you to believe before moving on. That you *can* do anything. Without that belief, the rest will not follow.

In ancient India, gurus would ask their students to take a *sankalpa*. In Sanskrit, this means an idea or notion formed in the heart or mind. It is also a solemn vow or stated determination to perform. In effect, it is a single-point focused resolve to do something. It is now your turn to take a sankalpa to perform.

Unlearn

It was the great scientist, Albert Einstein, who defined insanity as 'doing the same thing over and over again and expecting different results.' Unfortunately, that's precisely what most people do when studying. My attempt is to break the repetitive cycle of mistakes that you may be making.

Let's say that you wish to learn something new. For example, you usually write English and use the Roman script and now wish to learn how to write Urdu using the Nastaliq script. You are familiar with writing from left to right but for Urdu you have to write from right to left. In addition, you need to learn entirely new letters of the alphabet and strokes. To a certain extent, you almost need to 'unlearn' the instinctive urge to write from left to right. The writer and futurist Alvin Toffler insightfully said that 'The illiterates of the 21st century will not be those who cannot read or write. They will be the ones who cannot learn, unlearn and relearn.'

Think about what I'm offering you as that entirely new writing process. It is my aim to equip you to study far more effectively than you have ever done in the past. In order to learn the new method, you will necessarily need to let go of the stuff that hasn't worked so far for you.

Smart, not hard

We have all seen some classmates who breeze through their lessons, are hardly seen studying, have free time, enjoy extra-curricular and social activities ... and yet get good marks. How do they do it? I will attempt to reveal the efficient methods used by them in this book.

You may well ask: Why have we not been taught these methods in school? What I have found is that teachers and parents always advise students to study hard, but do not really tell them *how*. How to study smart rather than study hard is what this book attempts to reveal to you. Let me explain the difference with a short story.

Once upon a time there was a king who had three sons. The king was getting older and decided that it was time to choose a successor. The ageing monarch called all his sons and gave them a task. Each one was to fill a room with a single substance in such a way that not even the slightest gap would be left unfilled. They were allotted a few hours to achieve this.

All three princes hurried off in the directions of their respective rooms. The first decided to fill his room with large stones. He ordered his servants to start carrying out the task, but it was physically demanding work and progress was slow.

The second prince struck upon a better idea. He ordered his servants to fill the room with bales of hay. This was far easier than lifting heavy stones and the young prince succeeded in getting the entire room filled up within the allotted time.

The third prince simply took a small bottle filled with a liquid and carried it to the room allotted to him. He closed the windows and doors of the room and then sprinkled the liquid all over.

Once time had run out, the king visited all three rooms. The first room was only partially filled with stones. The problem was that due to the heavy nature of the work, the assignment had not been completed.

The second room was fully packed with hay. The problem was that the hay had tiny gaps through which sunlight could pass. This did not meet the criteria that the monarch had set.

The king visited the third room and as he opened the door, his nostrils were overpowered by the sweet fragrance of jasmine. The king visited every nook and cranny of the room and found that the smell of jasmine was all pervasive. He realized that the third prince had simply sprinkled perfume all over the room.

The king smiled. He had found an able successor. One who worked smart rather than hard.

Fine. So we need to work smart instead of hard. But how? Most people think that working smart means a 'short cut'. That's not quite true. Working smart means working in a manner that is organized, efficient and effective. Period.

1. Organized: How can you be better prepared for class, come under no last-minute pressure for assignments and work according to a planned schedule?
2. Efficient: How can you use your time in a way that promotes maximum learning in minimum time?
3. Effective: How can your organization and efficiency lead you to better learning and higher marks?

We must also remember that getting good marks is not enough. Studying without understanding is like chanting mantras in prayer without understanding the meaning or significance of those prayers. Why should those chants work for you if you can't even understand them? And *that* is also the difference between getting good marks and getting a good education.

Before we proceed further …

Unless you hold the belief that you *can* indeed make good marks happen, the rest will not follow. You also need to unlearn methods and techniques that have not worked for you so far. Finally, you need to learn how to work smart rather than hard. Understand these three elements completely before you go to the next step of this book.

STEP 2: FAIL TO PLAN = PLAN TO FAIL

Imagine this situation: A wealthy uncle dies and leaves you one crore rupees in his will—but with one condition. You must spend the entire amount in any manner that you like—within the span of one day. Any money remaining unspent after twenty-four hours will be taken away. You are not permitted to save the money or bank it. How will you spend it? Or will you let it go waste?

I imagine that you would start with a dream list: The latest top-end laptop, a high-end smart phone, designer clothes and accessories, motorbike or car, jewellery, parties, gifts (possibly some for your parents and siblings), investments or property purchases, charitable donations … You would then look for retailers as well as look at prices. As an intelligent person who wants to extract the maximum benefit, you would also check if you have exceeded the budget or if any money is going unutilized. Right?

You have intelligently proven that planning is necessary for *any* task. Now replace the one crore rupees with the minutes in your life. You have been given the gift of a limited amount of time, which can neither be saved nor banked. You have to decide how best to use it—or lose it forever.

Eliminate the black holes

Just as you made detailed plans on how to spend one crore rupees in twenty-four hours, you need to make a record of how you currently spend the hours of your day. For most students, the day is usually spent in six ways:

1. Institutional time: Time spent in classes at school or college.
2. Personal time: Time required for eating, sleeping, bathing, ablutions, prayers and exercise.
3. Study time: Time needed for homework or revision.
4. Extra-curricular time: Time for reading, hobbies or sports.
5. Social time: Time spent with family and friends.
6. Black holes: Non-productive time spent web browsing, chatting, watching television, playing video games and smart phone usage.

How can you get more done? The answer lies in removing or minimizing the black holes as also saving time on other activities. For example, an acquaintance of mine reduced his shower time from nineteen minutes to seven minutes. A young man in my neighbourhood began listening to audio recordings of his lessons while commuting to and from college by bus. His sister stopped eating in front of the television and began having meals with her parents so that family time and eating time could overlap.

Set realistic goals

Canadian globetrotter Jean Béliveau walked 47,000 miles on foot during an eleven-year journey across sixty-four countries and six continents using fifty-four pairs of shoes. He undertook the trip to promote the objective of peace and non-violence towards kids. His journey is believed to be the longest uninterrupted circumnavigation on foot.

Jean Béliveau probably had an end-destination in mind when he started out, but had to break it down into daily targets of around twenty miles. It would have been ridiculous for him to try and achieve the entire journey in a day or even a year. Similarly, you must set your goals incrementally so that you do not end up dejected or disappointed.

Your goals must be sensible, precise, certifiable, rewarding and pertinent. What does all this mean?

1. Sensible: The goal should be realistic, for example, how many problems can a normal student realistically expect to solve in sixty minutes?
2. Precise: The goal should be exact, for example,

'Read the fourth chapter of the Physics textbook'. It cannot and should not be 'Read physics'.
3. Certifiable: It should be possible to clearly understand if and when the goal has been achieved.
4. Rewarding: Each goal should be attached to a small or big reward. For example, an hour of maths problems entitles you to fifteen minutes of television.
5. Pertinent: The goal should be important and relevant. Studying for a class test that carries a substantive grade is more important than an assignment that does not.

Semester or term plan, weekly plan and daily plan

You should prepare a plan for the entire term or semester at the beginning of the period. Start with hours that are blocked for classes in school or college. Next, add some hours of study time for each day. Finally, plug in all other activities that need your time—exercise, sleep, extra-curricular activities or family time.

Next, the syllabus that you need to cover during the term or semester should be listed. These are the areas that you will cover during the hours that have been allocated as study time in your plan.

Remember to provide for free time in your schedule. Everything cannot be scheduled; the reason why schedules fail is precisely because they are over-packed. Also remember to allocate revision time according to your alertness cycle. Some people are more alert in the early hours of the morning whereas others perform better in the late hours of the night. Only you know what works for you.

Your semester or term plan should look something like the plan shown on pages 14 and 15. You will notice that time in school or college, time required for revision or homed for sleep, meals, hobbies or relaxation are meticulously plotted into the plan.

This particular term plan has been made on Microsoft Excel but you could use a manual alternative such as a simple chart paper on your wall or you could use more sophisticated tools online.

Next, your semester or term plan should result in a daily task list. I have found that the best way to make such a plan is by maintaining a diary in which each day of the year has a separate page, like the one shown on page 16.

Remember that each item from the syllabus requires different types of preparation at different stages. For example, refining class notes, completing homework assignments, reviewing what was taught in class and revising or practising for exams.

Effectively, your daily task list should have four sections. The first quarter of the page should list homework tasks.

	April	6AM	7AM	8AM	9AM	10AM	11AM	12PM	1PM	2PM
Mon	1	Pree-Class Review	Travel Time	Math Class	English Class	History Class	Physics Lab	Lunch Break	Geography Class	Economics Class
Tue	2	Pree-Class Review	Travel Time	Chemistry lab	Biology Class	Hindi Class	Economics Class	Lunch Break	Math Class	History Class
Wed	3	Pree-Class Review	Travel Time	Physics Class	History Class	Math Class	Biology Class	Lunch Break	Economics Class	Geography Class
Thu	4	Pree-Class Review	Travel Time	Biology Lab	Geography Class	Math Class	English Class	Lunch Break	Hindi Class	Chemistry Class
Fri	5	Pree-Class Review	Travel Time	English Class	Hindi Class	Chemistry lab	Math Class	Lunch Break	Economics Class	Physics Class
Sat	6	Sleep...	Sleep...	Revision Time	Revision Time	Revision Time	Revision Time	Lunch with Mom	Free Time	Free Time
Sun	7	Sleep...	Sleep...	Revision Time	Revision Time	Revision Time	Revision Time	Family Lunch	Family Time	Free Time
Mon	8	Pree-Class Review	Travel Time	Math Class	English Class	History Class	Physics Lab	Lunch Break	Geography Class	Economics Class
Tue	9	Pree-Class Review	Travel Time	Chemistry lab	Biology Class	Hindi Class	Economics Class	Lunch Break	Math Class	History Class
Wed	10	Pree-Class Review	Travel Time	Physics Class	History Class	Math Class	Biology Class	Lunch Break	Economics Class	Geography Class
Thu	11	Pree-Class Review	Travel Time	Biology Lab	Geography Class	Math Class	English Class	Lunch Break	Hindi Class	Chemistry Class
Fri	12	Pree-Class Review	Travel Time	English Class	Hindi Class	Chemistry lab	Math Class	Lunch Break	Economics Class	Physics Class
Sat	13	Sleep...	Sleep...	Revision Time	Revision Time	Revision Time	Revision Time	Lunch with Mom	Free Time	Free Time
Sun	14	Sleep...	Sleep...	Revision Time	Revision Time	Revision Time	Revision Time	Family Lunch	Family Time	Free Time
Mon	15	Pree-Class Review	Travel Time	Math Class	English Class	History Class	Physics Lab	Lunch Break	Geography Class	Economics Class
Tue	16	Pree-Class Review	Travel Time	Chemistry lab	Biology Class	Hindi Class	Economics Class	Lunch Break	Math Class	History Class
Wed	17	Pree-Class Review	Travel Time	Physics Class	History Class	Math Class	Biology Class	Lunch Break	Economics Class	Geography Class
Thu	18	Pree-Class Review	Travel Time	Biology Lab	Geography Class	Math Class	English Class	Lunch Break	Hindi Class	Chemistry Class
Fri	19	Pree-Class Review	Travel Time	English Class	Hindi Class	Chemistry lab	Math Class	Lunch Break	Economics Class	Physics Class
Sat	20	Sleep...	Sleep...	Revision Time	Revision Time	Revision Time	Revision Time	Lunch with Mom	Free Time	Free Time
Sun	21	Sleep...	Sleep...	Revision Time	Revision Time	Revision Time	Revision Time	Family Lunch	Family Time	Free Time
Mon	22	Pree-Class Review	Travel Time	Math Class	English Class	History Class	Physics Lab	Lunch Break	Geography Class	Economics Class
Tue	23	Pree-Class Review	Travel Time	Chemistry lab	Biology Class	Hindi Class	Economics Class	Lunch Break	Math Class	History Class
Wed	24	Pree-Class Review	Travel Time	Physics Class	History Class	Math Class	Biology Class	Lunch Break	Economics Class	Geography Class
Thu	25	Pree-Class Review	Travel Time	Biology Lab	Geography Class	Math Class	English Class	Lunch Break	Hindi Class	Chemistry Class
Fri	26	Pree-Class Review	Travel Time	English Class	Hindi Class	Chemistry lab	Math Class	Lunch Break	Economics Class	Physics Class
Sat	27	Sleep...	Sleep...	Revision Time	Revision Time	Revision Time	Revision Time	Lunch with Mom	Free Time	Free Time
Sun	28	Sleep...	Sleep...	Revision Time	Revision Time	Revision Time	Revision Time	Family Lunch	Family Time	Free Time

	April	3PM	4PM	5PM	6PM	7PM	8PM	9PM	10PM	...
Mon	1	Travel Time	Homework Time	Revision Time	GYM	Revision Time	Dinner	Reading Time	Sleep...	
Tue	2	Guitar Class	Travel Time	Homework Time	Coaching Class	Revision Time	Dinner	Reading Time	Sleep...	
Wed	3	House Games	Travel Time	Homework Time	GYM	Revision Time	Dinner	Reading Time	Sleep...	
Thu	4	Travel Time	Homework Time	Revision Time	Coaching Class	Revision Time	Dinner	Reading Time	Sleep...	
Fri	5	Travel Time	Homework Time	Revision Time	GYM	Revision Time	Dinner	Reading Time	Sleep...	
Sat	6	Football Club	Coaching Class	Movie	Movie	Movie	Dinner	Reading Time	Sleep...	
Sun	7	Free Time	Free Time	Guitar Class	Free Time	Free Time	Dinner	TV	Sleep...	
Mon	8	Travel Time	Homework Time	Revision Time	GYM	Revision Time	Dinner	Reading Time	Sleep...	
Tue	9	Guitar Class	Travel Time	Homework Time	Coaching Class	Revision Time	Dinner	Reading Time	Sleep...	
Wed	10	House Games	Travel Time	Homework Time	GYM	Revision Time	Dinner	Reading Time	Sleep...	
Thu	11	Travel Time	Homework Time	Revision Time	Coaching Class	Revision Time	Dinner	Reading Time	Sleep...	
Fri	12	Travel Time	Homework Time	Revision Time	GYM	Revision Time	Dinner	Reading Time	Sleep...	
Sat	13	Football Club	Coaching Class	Movie	Movie	Movie	Dinner	Reading Time	Sleep...	
Sun	14	Free Time	Free Time	Guitar Class	Free Time	Free Time	Dinner	TV	Sleep...	
Mon	15	Travel Time	Homework Time	Revision Time	GYM	Revision Time	Dinner	Reading Time	Sleep...	
Tue	16	Guitar Class	Travel Time	Homework Time	Coaching Class	Revision Time	Dinner	Reading Time	Sleep...	
Wed	17	House Games	Travel Time	Homework Time	GYM	Revision Time	Dinner	Reading Time	Sleep...	
Thu	18	Travel Time	Homework Time	Revision Time	Coaching Class	Revision Time	Dinner	Reading Time	Sleep...	
Fri	19	Travel Time	Homework Time	Revision Time	GYM	Revision Time	Dinner	Reading Time	Sleep...	
Sat	20	Football Club	Coaching Class	Movie	Movie	Movie	Dinner	Reading Time	Sleep...	
Sun	21	Free Time	Free Time	Guitar Class	Free Time	Free Time	Dinner	TV	Sleep...	
Mon	22	Travel Time	Homework Time	Revision Time	GYM	Revision Time	Dinner	Reading Time	Sleep...	
Tue	23	Guitar Class	Travel Time	Homework Time	Coaching Class	Revision Time	Dinner	Reading Time	Sleep...	
Wed	24	House Games	Travel Time	Homework Time	GYM	Revision Time	Dinner	Reading Time	Sleep...	
Thu	25	Travel Time	Homework Time	Revision Time	Coaching Class	Revision Time	Dinner	Reading Time	Sleep...	
Fri	26	Travel Time	Homework Time	Revision Time	GYM	Revision Time	Dinner	Reading Time	Sleep...	
Sat	27	Football Club	Coaching Class	Movie	Movie	Movie	Dinner	Reading Time	Sleep...	
Sun	28	Free Time	Free Time	Guitar Class	Free Time	Free Time	Dinner	TV	Sleep...	

> **FRIDAY**
> **03**
> **JANUARY**
>
> Homework tasks
> Read pages 29-37 of history
> Solve all maths problems at end of chapter 6
> write essay on Newton's laws of motion
>
> Revision tasks
> Review class notes from today in chemistry
> Re-solve problems given by Naresh sir for maths in class
> Active read the two chapters covered in Geography
>
> Preparation tasks
> preview chapter 4 in Economics
> go back to last year's microeconomics problem set
>
> Other tasks
> pick up A4 paper for term paper
> make copy of Sunil's notes from civics
> finish mom's errand
> Guitar class

> **SATURDAY**
> **04**
> **JANUARY**

The next quarter should list revision tasks pertaining to lessons that were taught that day. The third quarter should be preparation tasks pertaining to what is likely to be taught in class the following day. The last quarter is for all other tasks that need to be performed in the day.

Once exams start approaching, you should also make a calendar for the entire period during which you plan to cover the revision of your syllabus. This should be pasted on your wall or pinned on a corkboard.

It is your responsibility to ensure that your plan is realistic and achievable. It's important to schedule everything into the final day's plan—eating, exercise, dressing, commuting, classes, homework, revision and extra-curricular activities.

Plan, but with flexibility

Seriously attempt to treat your schedule as inviolable, but don't be afraid to deviate from the plan sometimes to study more for an upcoming exam. Planning can never be rigid. It has to be flexible.

Think of your plan as an optimal GPS route taking you from one place to another. The route may require you to take a flyover when you leave home, but if an accident has clogged up the flyover, you may need to re-route through narrow roads to reach your destination on time, even though the map says otherwise.

Prioritize tasks

The diary page will effectively become a 'To-Do' list for the day. This could include refining the notes that you took in school and reviewing them, completing homework assignments or reading material in preparation for a future class. Each of these tasks should be prioritized.

But what exactly is prioritization? It is simply a way of deciding the order in which tasks may be performed. Let me give you an example:

Imagine that you have an empty bucket before you. You also have some big rocks that can fill the bucket, as well as some pebbles, sand and water.

You put the big rocks in the bucket up to its brim. Is the bucket full?

Next you put the pebbles in the spaces around the big rocks. Now is the bucket full?

You now pour in the sand and give the bucket a shake? Is the bucket full as yet?

Finally you pour the water in. Indeed, now it is full.

The point is this: Unless you started by putting the big rocks in first, followed by the pebbles, then the sand and finally the water, you would not have succeeded in putting everything in. Moral of the story? Plan time-slots for the critical subjects and assignments before anything else. Those are the big rocks.

I have found that a simple way of prioritizing is by using a strategy employed by the thirty-fourth American President, Dwight Eisenhower. Simply put all your tasks into a matrix like the one on the next page.

If a task is important as well as urgent, then it must be given the highest priority and done now. For example, a homework assignment that needs to be submitted tomorrow. If a task is important but not urgent, then that should be given the next highest priority and scheduled. For example, revising something taught in

		IMPORTANT	
		YES	NO
URGENT	YES	NOW	DELEGATE
	NO	SCHEDULE	DISCARD

class earlier that day. If a task is not important yet urgent, find a way to delegate it. For example, a friend needs help with a homework assignment. Instead of getting involved personally, maybe you could refer him to a YouTube video that explains the key issues. Finally, if a task is neither urgent nor important, discard it. It is clogging up your valuable time.

Use spare time wisely

I often find that students do not use their time in school or college effectively. For example, a lecture is cancelled and one has an hour to spare before the next class. Most students gravitate towards the canteen or begin to fiddle with their mobile devices. Instead, a quick trip to the library or an opportunity to brush up on material that was taught the previous day would be a better use of the time.

Yes, you did make a semester plan which has several one-hour or thirty-minute blocks of time for studying. But there are bound to be a few minutes that are not as neatly structured. For example, ten minutes between two consecutive lectures or the time spent at the bus stop waiting for the bus to arrive. You can use this time wisely by carrying your flash cards (discussed later in this book). These can enable you to revise material during those little nuggets of free time. Remember one thing. Your most valuable resource is time. Use every free minute effectively.

Before we proceed further …

Benjamin Franklin famously said, 'If you fail to plan, you are planning to fail.' Ensure that your academic calendar is plotted out in advance. Maintain a daily 'To-Do' list of tasks to be performed and use a simple system to decide which tasks need to be given higher priority. You will see the difference in your own performance after you do this.

STEP 3: MAKE CLASSES COUNT

Why do most of us find classes and lectures boring?

The average teacher delivers lessons for average students and with much repetition at around 50 words per minute (wpm). Hardly any student is exactly average, so hardly any student is in sync with the teacher's pace. Your mind processes information at about 1000 wpm while the lecture is plodding along at 50 wpm.

To compensate, your mind processes other thoughts and observations, often completely missing the lesson. Your eyes drift to the window to gaze outside. You stare at other students in the room in order to see what they are doing. Your mind wanders to your last vacation and the fun you had. Before you even know it, class is over and you walk away, having absorbed nothing of what was said.

It is important that you find ways to extract value from your classroom experience. Here are a few tips that can guide you.

Prepare for class in advance

It is said that Arjuna, the greatest archer of the Mahabharata, practised archery in total darkness even before his guru had started to teach it. In effect, he was so dedicated that he was way ahead of his syllabus.

According to a law school graduate, this is the most important tip that helped get him through the torture of law school. He believes that if you pre-read the textbook or distributed notes for an upcoming class, when the material is actually presented in class, it will be the second time that you are exposed to it. This will not only make it easier to follow the class, but will also be an advantage when you eventually prepare for exams. Basically, you need to familiarize yourself with the lesson *before* it is taught in class. So prepare for tomorrow's lesson by reading it today from your textbook, working out the examples and noting your doubts.

If tomorrow's lesson depends on something you learnt last year but are not confident about, revise that lesson too. By doing this, you will have built up momentum for the lesson. You will now be in sync with the lesson when it is taught in class, and will be able to better understand, follow and appreciate it.

The front row actually does help

I remember that most students who sat in the front row of my college were considered 'uncool'. The cool chaps were usually the backbenchers. The problem is that when you are seated at the back, everything that every other student is doing in the rows ahead of you becomes the focus of your attention. It's a good idea to be in the front row (or the first few rows) simply to prevent distractions by curtailing your field of vision to the blackboard and teacher. The location makes it easier to hear the teacher as well as to see material on the blackboard, whiteboard or projection screen. Sitting in the direct gaze of the professor also means that you will tend to look around less and are also unlikely to leave class early.

Windows and doors are often a distraction, so try and be seated away from them. This can usually be achieved by choosing a place that is broadly in the centre of a given row.

Clarify doubts, adjust pace, participate

There is a Chinese proverb that the person who asks a question is a fool for five minutes, but the one who doesn't, remains a fool permanently. I have found that some students are reluctant to ask questions for fear of appearing stupid. Remember: There are no stupid questions. The stupidity, if any, lies in not adequately using the opportunity in class to clarify a genuine doubt. In any case, if you have prepared in advance for the class, the possibility of your question being shallow is miniscule.

Of course, different teachers have varying rules about taking questions. For example, some professors want to cover the material first, then take questions towards the end of the class. Make sure that you follow the guidelines of the teacher.

Also, if the lesson is moving at a pace that is too fast for you, do not hesitate to politely ask the professor to slow down or repeat. It can often be hard to judge the appropriate pace for a class, and most teachers are usually happy to accommodate requests as long as they know that the concerned student is sincere.

Try to actively participate in class. Such participation forces your mind to focus on the material being taught. A happy bonus is that it demonstrates to the teacher that you actually care about what is being taught (which means that you may catch a lucky break on the occasions when you need it).

Avoid talkative friends

You should let your classmates know that you are not to be spoken to during the lecture. There is enough time available to chat after class. If you find that a particular classmate is incorrigible, please move or privately request your teacher to change your location. Mark Twain correctly observed that 'If we were supposed to talk more than we listen, we would have two mouths and one ear.'

Impressions count

It is always a good idea to make a good impression on your teacher. Students who demonstrate that they care about their studies are often treated far differently to those who don't. Sometimes this difference can even reflect in grades. Remember, your teachers are human beings and can be swayed.

Talking to the students of previous batches about the likes and dislikes of your teacher is usually a good strategy. All teachers are made differently. While some like active participation, others prefer silence. While some prefer short and to-the-point answers in test papers, others prefer essay length and elaborate answers. Learning about your teachers' specific preferences can give you a competitive advantage.

Be punctual

Be on time for class. In fact, reach early. Students who arrive late can be an irritant for the teacher because of the distraction that they cause. In addition, such latecomers may not be able to keep up, owing to the fact that they missed out on some material.

Don't miss classes

One very basic point: Don't miss classes. Each class is like a brick in a wall that is being built from ground up. And a missing brick at the lower levels can affect the stability of the entire wall. Each class is a building block and it is vital that none of these blocks should be missing.

If indeed you do miss a class, ensure that you follow up and find out what was covered. Get one or more of your friends to teach you the material and share his or her notes. As you will see later, having a network of friends that can help you is rather important.

Homework

Homework is a word that we are taught to hate from an early age, because it is seen as an intrusion on our personal time away from school or college. Let's put that aside for a moment. Homework assignments are usually handed out in sync with what is being taught in class. Usually, homework assignments reinforce the concepts that have already been discussed in class. By doing your homework on time, you are doing yourself a big favour.

You shall later see that a theory called *The Forgetting Curve* proves that if you review anything new that you have learnt within twenty-four hours of learning it, you prevent yourself from forgetting up to 80 per cent of what you learnt. Quite often, homework assignments do precisely that: Reinforce what was taught in class.

Value of making notes

Two professors, Henry Roediger and Mark McDaniel, at the Washington University in St. Louis along with author Peter Brown, have condensed the best study knowledge based on several published scientific papers in *Make It Stick: The Science of Successful Learning*. The top tip which they recommend to enable you to study successfully and with least effort is to make notes *by hand* (not on computers or handheld devices) and to pay attention to what one is noting down. Please note that the term used is *making* notes, not *taking* notes. Taking notes is almost the equivalent of jotting down what is dictated (from ears to hand to paper, without the matter really going through the brain). There is no engagement involved in the act. Making notes implies that you are listening, registering, and then noting in your own words as part of the act of learning.

Make notes or listen?

So should you make notes or just concentrate on the lectures? In some schools and colleges, students are discouraged from making notes when the teacher is explaining the lesson. The aim is to ensure that students understand the lesson, grasp the concept and then get doubts cleared.

In the event that an educational institution has a policy against making notes *in* class, you should immediately do so *after* class. Why? When we're listening to the teacher in the classroom, that part of our brain that handles listening and language is active. This part of the brain passes on some of this information to our memory but crucial information is treated in the same way as trivia. When we make notes, something different happens. As we write, we create spatial relationships in the pieces of information that we are recording. Now, spatial tasks are the responsibility of another part of the brain. When we write, we end up putting some thought into evaluating and ordering the information before us. That process of writing (and not the notes themselves) is what helps 'fix' learning more firmly in our minds.

Remember that good notes should *not* be:

1. Noting verbatim what is being said in class.
2. Highlighting or underlining passages in textbooks without thought.
3. Copying passages from the textbook into your notes.
4. Making notes of everything rather than selectively doing so.

Finally, don't be in a hurry to leave the classroom. When you rush, you miss out the opportunity to make sure that you didn't leave out anything important in your notes.

Paper and pen wins

Writing and drawing by hand are very powerful tools. When you make notes by hand, you are engaging your brain. This does not happen to the same extent with a keyboard or tablet. In 2014, *Psychological Science* published a study that found that students who made notes by hand did far better than students who used laptops, smart phones or tablets.

Zoom in

Zoom into what your teacher is saying. Look out for phrases like 'this is important' or 'please do not forget that'. If the professor says that something is important, the odds are that it is. Make a note of it by starring it so that you pay special attention to it when you are studying.

Diagrams

If a professor makes the effort of specifically drawing a diagram, chart or picture on the blackboard or whiteboard, there are chances that you may find it in your next exam. Always copy it into your notes.

Use abbreviations

While making notes in class, feel free to use abbreviations. This allows you to efficiently jot down words without taking too much time. You may develop your own abbreviation system, or use common ones like 'b/t' for between, 'w/o' for without, 'b/c' for because and 'y' or 'n' for yes and no. Maintain a master list of abbreviations that you use so that there is never a chance of being unable to decipher your notes later.

Keep them organized

The method by which you organize your notes is also very important. Some students maintain a separate notebook for each subject during class and then prepare fair notes (again, in separate notebooks) after class. Some use a ring binder with individual pieces of paper that they can collate after class. Some of the most organized students that I have observed even have separate folders for formulae, theorems, grammar rules or historical dates.

Be consistent in terms of how you make notes so that you will not have difficulty in understanding them later. If you find yourself unable to make good notes, find the one person in your class who seems to have a great system and find out how he or she does it.

Refine your notes

Making notes helps you in two ways. One, it helps you fix the material more firmly in your mind, as described above. Two, it helps you in your subsequent revision. Once you have made notes in class, you should refine those notes further at home. This automatically ensures that you end up reviewing the material within twenty-four hours!

Your notes should cover the most important takeaways from the class and should present the information in simple bullet points or charts. There is no point in having exhaustive notes. They defeat the very purpose of notes.

I remember maintaining very thin eighty-page notebooks, one for each subject. I would devote one side of one page to each lecture and by the end of the academic year, that notebook was the only study aid that I needed. While other students would be using various guides or coaching class notes, my handwritten notebooks did the job for me.

The 24-hour rule

Remember that once you are out of class, you will forget up to 80 per cent of the material that was presented to you during the lecture. This holds good even if you understood everything that was said. There is a catch, though. If you review or refine your notes later that day (within twenty-four hours of the lecture), the information will be stored in your long-term memory, not your short-term memory. (And if you have studied the lesson even before attending the lecture, you are streets ahead of the others!)

When you go over the material, make sure that you underline all the elements that you do not fully comprehend. Make an effort to research and find the relevant answers to these issues before you bring the day to a close. You will soon realize that preparation for exams will become a 'casual review' rather than 'studying' if you follow this twenty-four-hour rule.

Preview-View-Review

I started by telling you to prepare for class in advance so that you would be in a better position to absorb the lessons. I then told you to pay attention in class and make notes. I ended by telling you to review the material taught in class within twenty-four hours of the class and to refine your notes.

Remember this golden rule of preview-view-review. The American billionaire John D. Rockefeller was known to have said that 'The secret of success is to do the common things uncommonly well.' Well, the preview-view-review routine is one of those common things that you need to learn how to do uncommonly well.

Speak to your teacher

Shyness prevents many students from approaching their teachers. That's a mistake. Do not be afraid to ask about the nature of an upcoming test or the specific material that you should focus on. You will be surprised as to how many clues you can get from simply talking to your professor. Also, do not be afraid to ask for special help. Teachers always want to help students who are keen on the subject.

Before we proceed further …

Use the preview-view-review routine for all your classes. Prepare for class in advance. Pay attention in class. Do not be afraid to approach your teacher in or after class. Make notes, keep them organized and refine them. Use the twenty-four-hour rule to revise material that has been taught. Be punctual, don't miss classes and avoid talkative friends. Participate in class and strike the right impression with your teachers.

STEP 4: BE CONSISTENT AFTER CLASS

Ever heard of Joe Girard? He has been called the world's greatest salesman by the *Guinness Book of World Records*. One of the important teachings from Girard is: 'The elevator to success is out of order. You'll have to use the stairs! One step at a time.'

Girard has simply reiterated the fundamental rule that there is no substitute for consistent work. In similar vein, the Roman poet and philosopher Lucretius said that drops of rain make a hole in a stone not by violence, but by falling on it repeatedly.

The Japanese have a concept called *Kaizen*. It is a Sino-Japanese word that means 'change for the better'. This fundamental principle has been used by Japanese industry to apply continuous and constant incremental improvement of working practices *every day*. This is the ideal way to think of consistency. So, let me start this step by narrating a story that conveys the idea perfectly:

A young boy in China came from his remote village to become a monk at the world-renowned Shaolin Temple.

The Shaolin monks were known worldwide for their skill in martial arts such as Kung-Fu. The boy was interviewed by a senior monk and was finally accepted.

On his very first day of instruction, he was ordered by his teacher to carry a heavy wooden bucket down the mountainside to a stream, fill it entirely with water and bring it back into the temple courtyard. The boy did as he was told, but found that it required a lot of effort on his part to carry the heavy bucket all the way back to the temple. When he got back, most of the water had splashed out. The instructor emptied out the remaining water and commanded the boy to do it again and ensure that he returned with the bucket full. The boy repeated the process and this time he managed to get most of the water back to the temple.

'Good,' observed the instructor. 'Now stand next to the bucket and with your palms slap the surface of the water. Keep doing it until there is no water left in the bucket.' After a few minutes, the boy's palms were red and burning from slapping the water, but he continued until all the water had splashed out.

'Excellent,' said the instructor. 'Now go fetch another bucket of water and do it again.' This went on the entire day, and to the boy's disappointment, the next day, too. Then the following day, and the next. Weeks and months went by and all that the boy did was carry several buckets of water to the courtyard and slap all the water out on each occasion. The boy felt that he was being

punished. He wondered why his teacher refused to teach him Kung-Fu.

After a year, the head monk called the boy into his office. 'You have been here for a year. I want you to take a break and visit your family. Please be back here in two weeks to resume your training.'

When the villagers heard that the young Shaolin monk was coming home, they were overjoyed. They led him to a banquet that had been laid out in his honour on a heavy stone table in the village courtyard. When they had eaten, the villagers asked him to demonstrate his Kung-Fu skills. He felt guilty and told them that did not want to do any demonstration. But they insisted. The boy felt humiliated because he had no skills to show.

'Leave me alone,' he yelled as he stood up from the table at which they were all seated. 'I learned absolutely nothing!' He slammed his hand down on the table in anger. Everyone was stunned.

They stood in pin-drop silence, staring at the thick stone table that the boy had broken when he slammed his hand down.

What is the point of the story? Simple, really. Consistently doing your revision and homework each day cannot be substituted by sudden cramming. There is power in consistency. Don't ever forget it. Remember the words of the author Robert Collier who said: 'Success is the sum of small efforts, repeated day in and day out.'

Refer to your daily plan

As decided earlier, you have all the tasks for the day noted in your diary. Prioritize these tasks and get cracking on them once you are in your study space.

Your pace is unique

Each student will read, absorb or do anything at a speed that is unique to him or her. Do not compare yourself to someone else. Determine a pace that works for you, then follow through. Some subjects or theories will come quicker to you while others will take longer. There is no such thing as an ideal pace. You are the only one who should be setting your pace. Bill Gates, the billionaire founder of Microsoft, once said, 'Most people overestimate what they can do in one year and underestimate what they can do in ten years.' Figure out your pace and stick with it.

Procrastination

It is said that the secret to getting ahead is simply getting started. Indeed we all know that there is one great spoiler that rears its head from time to time. It's called procrastination. Procrastination is the avoidance of completing an important task. It can involve:

1. Taking longer breaks than the time taken for tasks.
2. Giving top priority to least important tasks and vice versa.

3. Spending time on black hole activities such as social media, casual web browsing or instant messaging.
4. Starting a high priority task, then losing tempo by taking a break before completing it.
5. Waiting for the right mood or right time or guidance for difficult, unpleasant, unfamiliar or challenging tasks.
6. Not maintaining a daily to-do list, thus forgetting what needs to be accomplished.
7. Not prioritizing tasks using the Eisenhower rule.

When we procrastinate, we end up converting a molehill into a mountain of problems. The ill-effects of procrastination are described in this nursery rhyme:

For want of a nail the shoe was lost.
For want of a shoe the horse was lost.
For want of a horse the rider was lost.
For want of a rider the message was lost.
For want of a message the battle was lost.
For want of a battle the kingdom was lost.
And all for the want of a horseshoe nail.

Have you ever wondered why people who retire from the army, navy or air force are in demand by leading companies? It is primarily because of the discipline that is instilled into them while in the armed forces. The primary element of this training is learning to get things done without procrastination. Treat each subject and each concept within each subject as the horseshoe nail. And if you do, I can promise you that you will succeed in nailing it!

So what can you do to avoid becoming a habitual procrastinator?

1. Get into the habit of making a daily to-do list.
2. Use the Eisenhower system to prioritize your tasks.
3. Use the Pomodoro Technique to perform the tasks. This is described after this list.
4. Focus on one task at a time, without distractions. At such times, keep your mobile phone away.
5. Remind yourself of the unpleasant consequences of not completing the tasks that are on your list.
6. Visualize the sense of satisfaction that you will have once your tasks are completed. Imagine the pleasure of getting a high grade. Also imagine the pain that previous instances of procrastination inflicted upon you.
7. Start with a task that you consider the most unpleasant. Simply achieving that gives you a confidence boost.
8. Strike off completed tasks from your list, thus giving yourself a sense of achievement.
9. Reward yourself for completed tasks with a walk, snooze, drink, gym session or game. This is equally important.
10. Penalize yourself for not getting tasks completed. You decide what penalties work for you. But remember that for a penalty to truly achieve its purpose, you have to be hard on yourself.

Try the Pomodoro Technique

Once you have your daily study tasks planned out, you need to work with a system that will enable you to get your work done efficiently and effectively. The human mind cannot efficiently focus on any single task for too long. What's the solution?

Have you heard of the Pomodoro? This is a tomato-shaped timer that is often kept in kitchens to help monitor baking, freezing, toasting or roasting time.

Francesco Cirillo was inspired by this kitchen tool and created a technique known as the Pomodoro Technique in the 1980s. There are five basic steps to implement this technique:

1. Decide on the task.
2. Set your clock or timer to 25 minutes.
3. Work on the task for 25 minutes with zero distractions.

4. Take a break of 3–5 minutes after the task and then move on to the next task.
5. Complete 4 such tasks and then take a longer break of 15–30 minutes.

As tasks are split into smaller segments, they become more manageable. This is far less daunting than one mega task. Think of Jean Béliveau and the 47,000 miles he had to walk. Splitting that down into smaller chunks was the key in getting through the bigger task.

It has been proven that one's focus and concentration tend to decrease with time. A study on the ability of the human mind to focus on a particular matter—what is commonly called the attention span—reveals that our attention actually drops with time. You will notice from the graph below that there is a massive drop in human attention after thirty minutes or so.

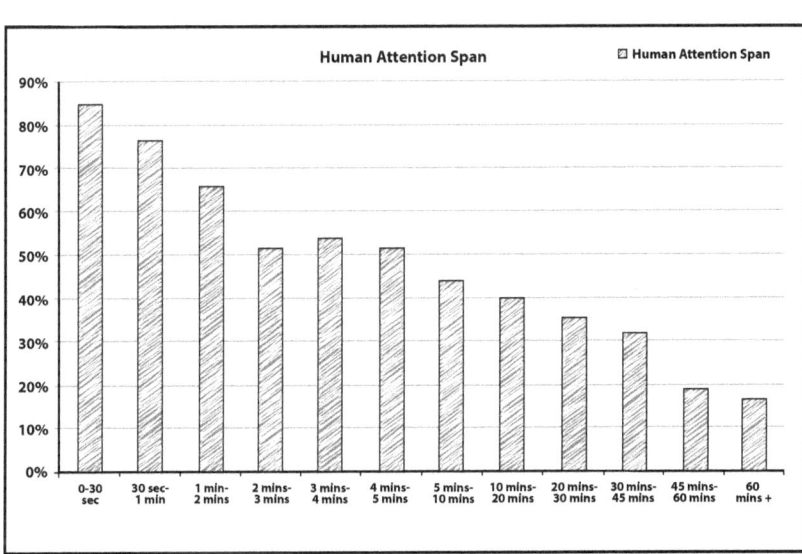

Hence the Pomodoro technique limits each working segment to twenty-five minutes, after which you reward yourself with a short break. During this break, you leave your study position, stretch, have a drink, visit the rest room, massage your temples or eyes, breathe deeply or walk around. The short break enables you to attack the next task with far more concentration. Longer breaks of fifteen to thirty minutes after four Pomodoro tasks can be used for taking a walk, a meal, a gym session or a power nap.

Think of the routine as chopping wood and the breaks as time taken to sharpen the blade of your axe. There's simply no point in expending more effort with a blunt blade.

Motivate yourself

Are you a self-starter, kick-starter, push-starter or a non-starter? Yes, this is inspired by motorbikes. We can classify people as:

'Self-starters' who study or work without having to be reminded or forced; 'kick-starters' and 'push-starters' need to be coerced, reminded and forced, after which they begin; no threats and coercion can make 'non-starters' work against their will. Each of us comes under different classifications at different times, and in different situations. The trick lies in self-motivation to become a self-starter at will—for the right tasks.

Once you have started, are engaged and involved, and have built up momentum, you will enjoy doing the job and facing challenges. The real prize is the thrill, the 'high' you will feel after successfully completing the job, and you may even enjoy doing it the next time having tasted success once. This is similar to a familiar subject being your favourite subject. You will now approach each new task as a challenge to be overcome, a new peak to be climbed. Yes, you will become a self-starter.

Multitasking is a bad idea

Think of your computer that slows down when multiple web pages and apps are open or running simultaneously. The machine is using too much RAM and the only way to speed it up is by closing down low priority RAM-guzzling applications.

Quite often you may think that you are using your time effectively by texting or messaging while studying, but the truth is that you are guzzling RAM on low priority activities. A study by the Indiana University has shown that multitasking interferes with the absorption and processing of information. Other studies by the Ohio State University and the Kaiser Family Foundation have also confirmed that attempting to multitask while studying is foolish.

Have you ever seen a paper ignited using a magnifying lens? One simply holds a magnifying glass in the sunlight in such a way that the sun's rays pass through it and converge on a specific spot on the paper placed below it. If you hold the lens and paper steady, the paper starts smoking and catches fire in a short time. This is the power of focused concentration. Focused study with no distractions and disturbances burns the lesson into your brain.

If you are thinking, 'Easy to say, but it is difficult to focus', I empathize (not sympathize) with you, and advise you to remember that, 'The mind is a monkey.' In other words, the human mind cannot efficiently focus on any single task for long (just as a monkey cannot stay still). But once the monkey (or mind) gets involved in a task, it continues the task. Just as a monkey can be trained to perform, you can train your mind to perform miracles by ignoring, reducing, removing and filtering out unwanted distractions and concentrating on the jobs to be done, one at a time. Once you become a self-starter, you will find yourself climbing the ladder of success! And once each lesson or challenge is successfully completed, you get a 'high' from your success, tick it off from your list, and are happy to say to yourself, 'One pending item less!'

It is said that after passing a test involving shooting the eye of a bird in a tree, Arjuna said he could see nothing except the eye of the bird while releasing his arrow. Such was his focus!

Variety boosts learning

Scientists have discovered that you can improve your learning by focusing on several distinct but related topics, rather than by concentrating on just one topic. Ideally, you should avoid studying the same subjects for too long. When you are tired of one subject, start another subject and avoid getting bored.

Create your study timetable taking this into account. Ideally, alternate between unrelated subjects, for example, a language followed by maths, then history, then physics. If memorizing vocabulary, throw in reading and comprehension as well.

If working on mathematics, try tackling several concepts instead of just one. Let's consider an oversimplified example. If one is doing ten problems that involve division, then each time that we approach the problem in that set, we already know that it involves division. On the other hand, if we take ten assorted problems that involve multiple functions such as division, multiplication, addition or subtraction, it means that we have to necessarily apply our minds to think about *which* operation needs to be performed (and this increases our alertness levels).

Endurance training

Endurance training is the act of exercising to increase one's endurance. The very word 'endurance' tells us something. Endurance is defined as the ability to bear an unpleasant or difficult process or situation without giving way. Thus we have seen movies in which athletes are pushed by their trainers a little further each day to increase their endurance. I believe that you can also apply endurance training to the act of studying. How?

First, prepare yourself for two learning tasks rather than one (say, solving maths problems and sentence construction in English). Second, begin working on one of the tasks. Third, if you find that your mind is drifting, decide to move on to the second task, but only after pushing yourself to do one more activity within the current task set. This is where endurance comes in. For example, if you have solved five problems in a set of ten problems, force yourself to do a sixth before you move on. Fourth, move on to the second task. Fifth, try your best to complete it, but if your mind drifts, push yourself to do one more sentence and go back to the first task. In effect, you will end up pushing yourself beyond what you are used to. This will be further enhanced over time.

Optimum recall

There is one trick related to learning that has been known to us since 1885, but neither teachers nor students seem to give it any importance. Based on a theory propounded in 1885 by Hermann Ebbinghaus, it is called *The Forgetting Curve*. Essentially, if you review anything new that you have learnt within twenty-four hours of learning it, you prevent yourself from forgetting up to 80 per cent of what you have learnt. After a week, it requires only five minutes to retain 100 per cent of the information.

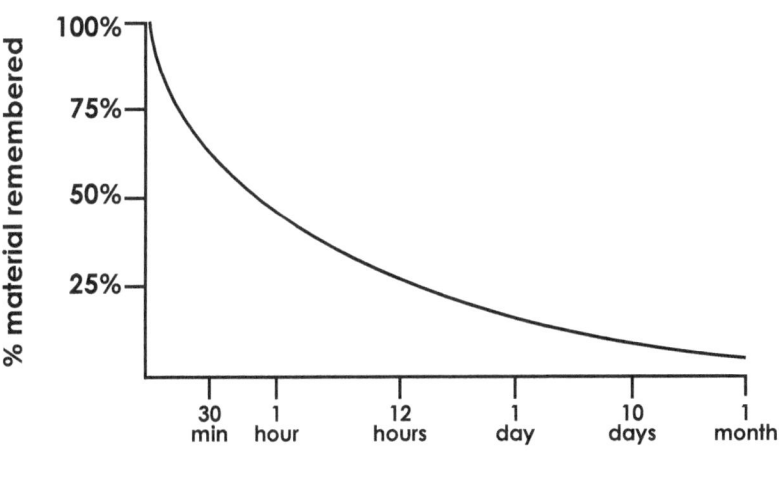

Time elapsed

How can you apply this? Let's imagine that you are in class and the lecture being delivered by the professor relates to an entirely unfamiliar concept. Now, if you simply review that very material within twenty-four hours, you will remember 80 per cent of what was taught. Psychologists at the University of California at San Diego have discovered that studying closer to the moment when you learned the material is better than studying closer to the time of the exam. In their opinion, the optimal time is at around 10 per cent of the time between learning and testing. So if you learnt something on Day 1 and the exam is on Day 30, you should revise it latest by Day 3.

Please take all the research findings that I present to you in this book with a healthy dose of scepticism. Studies show that it's enough for people to simply say 'studies show' to make the proposition magically acceptable. Don't fall into that trap!

Before we proceed further …

Refer to your daily task list and be consistent in your after-class routine. Be aware of the human tendency to procrastinate. Review all new material within twenty-four hours. Switch subjects to promote learning. Avoid multitasking. Use the Pomodoro technique to your advantage. Set your own unique pace.

STEP 5: MASTER THE SCIENCE OF READING

By reading their textbooks several times, many students wrongly believe that they know the material perfectly. Why? Because they are imagining this when the open book is right before their eyes.

This problem was outlined in a 2009 study published in the journal *Psychological Science* by a professor of psychology at Washington University in St. Louis. The study says that a better strategy is to read, then recall. In effect, you read the material once and close the book and hide your notes, if any. You then attempt to recall what you read with the book closed. Write it down or, if you like, say it out loud. This process called 'active recall' allows your brain to cement long-term memorization of the material.

If you can't do this, but still believe that you know your material, you are a victim of what I call the 'Repeated Reading' syndrome.

Let's go through some of the key points that can help you read and recall better.

Posture

Your posture while you read is exceptionally important. If you lie down on a couch (that you associate with watching television) or on your bed (that you associate with sleeping), how can you expect *not* to feel sleepy? Sit upright on a chair while reading. You could even choose to stand. What you need to avoid is slouching or using furniture that is designed for goofing off.

Questions first

If you are reading your textbook, even before you begin reading a chapter, quickly read the questions at the back of the chapter. The questions usually cover material that the textbook writers believe is important. Having read these questions, you will recognize the important concepts quickly when you get down to reading the chapter.

Try SQ3R

SQ3R is a reading and comprehension method that is named thus for its five steps—**S**urvey, **Q**uestion, **R**ead, **R**ecite, and **R**eview. The SQ3R method was introduced by Francis Pleasant Robinson in 1946.

The first step, surveying, involves skimming through the chapter, note headings, sub-headings and any other outstanding features such as figures, tables and summary paragraphs. This survey step should take three to five minutes only, and it prepares the reader for what will be presented. It is like looking at a map before you start driving towards a distant destination.

The second step, questioning, involves converting headings and sub-headings into questions and looking for answers in the context of the text. For example: What is this chapter about? What question is this chapter trying to answer? This step should also take three to five minutes, but it ensures that the reader will seek answers to key questions.

Next, use the background work done with 'S' and 'Q' in order to begin active reading. Active reading is different from reading. Active reading involves reading in a way as to answer the questions raised under 'Q'. On the other hand, passive reading is simply reading without engaging with the material.

The second 'R' refers to recitation. This means closing the book and attempting to recall the key issues discovered during active reading. The reader tries to retrieve the material from memory, almost like telling someone else about the information he has just read. The reader must use his or her own words to identify major points and provide answers to questions from the 'Q' step. This recitation step may be done either in an oral or written format and is critical in boosting long-term memory for the material.

The final step is reviewing. By this stage, the student should have a study sheet with keywords and phrases that emerged from the last step. This needs to be reviewed to ensure that the central theme, key questions and critical points have been absorbed.

Or use PQRST

This is almost the same as SQ3R but goes a little further. The PQRST method involves the following steps:

1. Preview
2. Question
3. Read
4. Self-recite
5. Test

First, preview the chapter by scanning it. This involves reading the chapter outline or summary at the beginning and giving some attention to the headings and subheadings of various sections and subsections. The aim is to get an overall idea of the key material that will be covered.

Second, question yourself by framing questions for yourself from the headings and subheadings of each section and subsection.

Third, read the chapter while alertly checking for answers to the questions that you framed in Step 2.

Fourth, close the book and try to remember the key points of each section or subsection. Possibly you could recite aloud to yourself. If you find yourself fumbling, return to Step 3.

Fifth, test yourself by attempting to answer the questions provided at the back of the chapter as also the questions that you had framed. It is important for you to understand how many of the key issues from the chapter you can recall.

Paper wins

Ebooks, web pages and YouTube are excellent add-ons in learning, but research findings still show that traditional print materials work better when it comes to studying. Research in America found that the iPad causes students to read 6.2 per cent slower than while reading a printed book. In effect, iPads are great for leisure reading, but not for studying.

Extending the research a little further, a study carried out in the University of Leicester in England discovered that students needed many more repetitions to learn new material on a computer screen than required with a printed book. So try and stick with printed books when it comes to studying.

Speed reading skills

Some students tend to believe that they can cover mountains of material towards examination time by using techniques such as speed reading. It is precisely because of this misplaced notion that I wish to provide you with some clarity on this subject.

We first learn by reading individual alphabets. We then progress to joining the alphabets to make words. Then words that join to make sentences which convey some meaning. Eventually, our brains learn to read sentences rather than individual words.

Did you read the sentence in the triangle? Did you notice that the word 'the' has been repeated? Most people miss out on the repeated word because they aren't reading words but sentences. In that sense, we are already practising speed reading.

Now, during our initial learning phase, we often need to read aloud. This is called vocalization. As our reading and language skills increase, we stop reading aloud, although some people continue to use their lips to silently outline each word. At the next stage, we stop using our lips, but still 'hear' each word mentally while reading it. This is called sub-vocalization. This improves our reading speed to about 150-200 wpm. Sub-vocalization has some advantages, but hampers reading speed.

Sub-vocalization helps one pronounce words, understand new concepts and languages. Thus, when you are reading your lessons for the first time, you necessarily need to read at your normal speed with sub-vocalization. Just as slow eating with chewing is preferred to gobbling, normal-paced reading with sub-vocalization is preferred to speed reading. But what about revision? That's where speed reading can really help.

It is true that the brain processes data at around 1,000 wpm and that our average reading speed is 150-200 wpm. It is thus no surprise that many find reading boring. You should ignore programmes and courses claiming that they can teach you how to read at 1,000 wpm. Instead, you could teach yourself to read faster than your usual speed using the methods outlined below.

You can make yourself read faster by using a finger, pointer or pencil to move under words slightly faster than your usual reading speed. You could even use a ruler or white paper and move it below the line you are reading and thus enhance your speed.

When you use this technique, you will instinctively make further progress and realize that you can ignore smaller words (a, an, and, the, of, on …) and still make sense of what you are reading. You are now reading chunks and blocks. This practice should be continued until you do not need the pointer and are naturally able to read at about 400-500 wpm *with retention intact*. This sort of speed reading is what you should aim for. It is great for subsequent revisions after the material has already been 'learnt' earlier. Do not substitute your regular, sub-vocalized reading with this sort of speed reading when you are reading the material for the first or second time. Remember, you have yet to 'learn' it.

Also, when you read, do not forget to blink. It keeps your eyes from getting fatigued, and the information you just read is processed by the brain during these blinks. Keeping the book at a slightly greater distance enables you to use your peripheral vision; your eyes are able to scan greater areas and see more words with less eye movement. Since you are challenging yourself to read faster, your mind is less distracted, and you absorb more information from your reading. Underlining or highlighting the main parts of your lessons in advance will be useful while speed reading just before your exams.

If you feel that speed reading is difficult, please realize that you are already practising speed reading in daily life when you are reading road signs, GPS directions, scrolling text and subtitles in movies. If you are wondering if it is worth the effort, it is like choosing between a bullock cart and a bullet train. You can decide and choose for yourself.

But remember, speed reading skills need to be worked on. The famous Hollywood actor Woody Allen once joked about speed reading thus: 'I took the speed reading course and then finished novel *War and Peace* in 20 minutes. It's about Russia.'

Speed reading at 1,000 wpm is a scam. But speed reading at 400-500 wpm is not. You can accomplish it if you actually work on developing this skill.

Use the highlighter

As you read, you should highlight, underline or circle 'keywords' or key phrases to keep your brain fully focussed. If the passage that you are reading is very intense, there is no harm in finding alternative words for the difficult ones and noting them in the margins. The very process of finding an alternative word or phrase can help the idea sink in.

It's always a good idea to use a highlighter or to underline the most relevant points in the body of the text so that it becomes far easier to spot them when you do a subsequent review, possibly at exam time.

It is important to be selective when highlighting, because too much highlighting defeats its very purpose.

Making your own notes in pencil in the margins of the text to summarize or draw attention is also a good idea. All of this can help the main points sink in. If you are not allowed to make notes in the margins because the books in question are shared, you can use sticky notes.

Master the keywords

Whenever you read a chapter in your textbook, you will realize that one particular word (or phrase) within a paragraph can effectively communicate the essence of that paragraph. By building a list of such keywords or phrases, you should be in a position to expand on them during an exam. Think of a keyword as a collapsible umbrella that occupies minimal space when folded but can be opened to full size when needed.

It is also important to study the critical words used in a chapter. Whenever a concept is introduced, there is usually a special term that describes it. This could very well become your keyword. More importantly, utilizing that term in your exam answers ensures that the grader knows that you *really* know your stuff.

Read aloud

This approach can slow down your reading but substantially improve your absorption. This is particularly true for words and phrases that are difficult or utterly boring or challenging, like a new language.

I remember that the word 'platyhelminthes' in my biology class was a mouthful. I would repeat it aloud while reading. Once you no longer fear the word and know how to pronounce it, recalling it becomes easier.

Select the best sources for study materials

I have seen many students searching for textbooks other than the recommended ones. That's a bad idea. The books prescribed in your syllabus are the ones used in class, the ones used in prescribing homework and the ones used in setting question papers. You are doing yourself no favours by stepping outside.

Some schools and colleges also provide summarized versions of textbooks, notes that have been optimized for retention, mnemonics collections, and key problem sets (along with answers). If available, please use them. Do yourself a favour by not attempting to reinvent the wheel.

ADHD and Dyslexia

Often, schools are unable to tell that a student who is inattentive, distracted or having difficulties with reading or writing, may actually have Attention Deficit Hyperactivity Disorder (ADHD), dyslexia, or both. There are many students who go through school being told that they are lazy or stupid simply because the institution is unable to recognize a learning disability.

Almost one in four students with ADHD is also diagnosed with dyslexia. Between 15 per cent and 40 per cent of students with dyslexia also have ADHD. These days there are evaluation tests, specialized reading and writing routines, medication as well as therapy that can deal with these conditions. The key challenge lies in being able to recognize them.

Before we proceed further ...

Pay attention to your posture while reading. Use either SQ3R or PQRST while reading. Using paper for note-taking instead of electronic material helps. Speed reading can help you in your revision. Use a highlighter and make notes in the margin. Read aloud for better absorption. Master the keywords or phrases. Use the prescribed study materials rather than others.

STEP 6: BOOST YOUR MEMORY QUOTIENT

There are those who say that studying is about understanding, not memorizing. Frankly, that's a lie. Studying is about understanding *and* memorizing. Even with practice subjects such as maths or physics, you do need to memorize the formulae or key concepts, then apply them to solving problems. It is thus foolish to discount the value of memorization.

Memorization happens in three stages: Registration, Retention and Recall. Registration is the act of becoming aware of the information. For example, someone shares a phone number with you. The second stage is retention. At this stage you decide consciously whether you wish to retain the information or not and, if so, for how long. Recall is the final stage, where you exercise your grey cells to retrieve the information, thus further strengthening the memory.

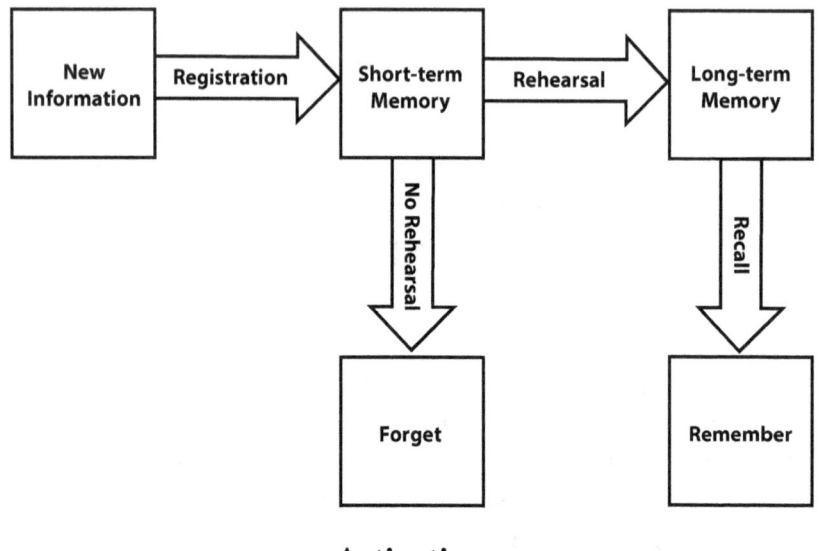

Activating

Before you even open your book to a given chapter, you should do what is called 'activation'. Let's assume that you are starting a new topic. Odds are that you already know a little bit about it. Before you start studying, take a pen and paper and jot down anything that you *think* you already know, in very brief points. Why should you do this? Simple. The strongest memories are those that are attached or 'hooked' to things that you already know.

For example, you are about to study the reign of the Mughal emperor, Akbar. Chances are that you already have some rudimentary factoids associated with him. When you jot these down before starting to study, you are actually nailing hooks into the wall. You will be able to hang your clothes (your actual learning) on these hooks later.

The Forgetting Curve

As mentioned earlier, *The Forgetting Curve* tells us that if you review anything new that you have learnt within twenty-four hours of learning it, you retain up to 80 per cent of what you learnt. After a week it requires only five minutes to retain 100 per cent of the information. So do yourself a favour and take advantage of this each day.

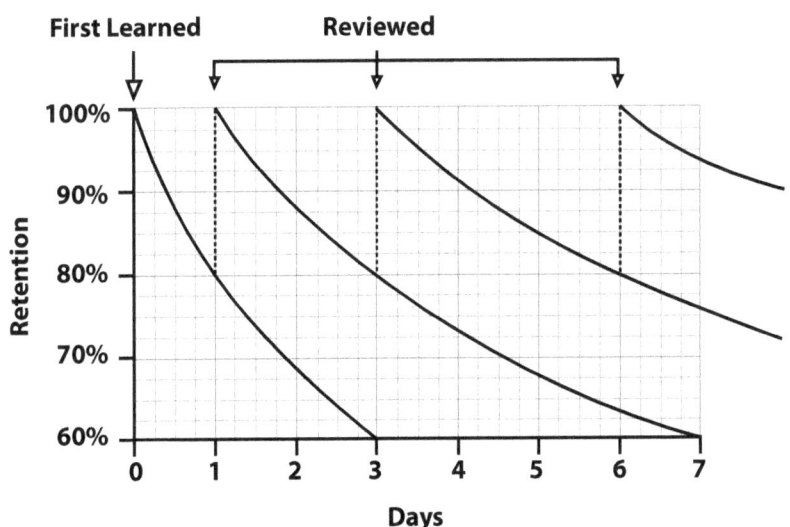

Hermann Ebbinghaus' theory (1885) shows that each repetition in learning increases the optimum interval before the next repetition is needed (for near-perfect retention, initial repetitions need to be made within days, but later they can be after years). From the diagram above, we see that every additional review increases the number of days that the memory is retained.

The best way of planning your review is:

1. Review the material immediately after the lecture.
2. Then repeat the review after one hour.
3. Then after one day.
4. Then after one week.
5. And finally after one month.

Mind maps

Mind maps are diagrams used to visually organize information. Normally a mind map is created around a single concept drawn as an image in the centre of a blank page, then associated representations of ideas are added around it. Major ideas branch out from the central concept, and other ideas from major ideas. They are also like roots or branches coming from the main trunk. Even though the basic concept of a mind map has been in existence for a long time, the idea was firmly brought into the world of learning in the Seventies by a book called *Use Your Head* by Tony Buzan.

According to Khurshed Batliwala and Dinesh Ghodke, in their book *Ready, Study, Go: Smart Ways to Learn*, there are six Cs involved in mind maps—**C**entral idea, **C**onciseness, **C**raziness, **C**urves, **C**olours and **C**artoons. Let's say that the central idea is 'writing skills'. Then one could branch out from that central idea to cover spelling, grammar, expression or content. Each of these concisely described nodes could be further branched out. For example, grammar could be branched out into verbs, adjectives, adverbs, nouns, pronouns and so on.

Our brains like visual images. The left half of the brain thinks linearly, following direct linkages to related ideas. On the other hand, the right half of the brain likes to see the whole picture, preferably with colours and flow. A mind map bridges that gap between both sides of the brain and is thus an excellent way of storing and memorizing information.

The authors suggest that one should use curves for the branches because our brain loves curves. They also suggest that we should be playfully crazy in drawing such mind maps, because slightly crazy elements make the map easier to recall. Colours help categorize the information and make it easier to remember. The authors also suggest making crazy doodles on the paper so as to make the map more distinctive.

Given below is an example of a mind map that explores the subject of tennis. Notice the curved connectors, the crazy fonts and the imagery (even though you can't observe the colours in this black-and-white book). It is all of these elements that make the mind map memorable, thus enhancing our ability to recall the individual elements.

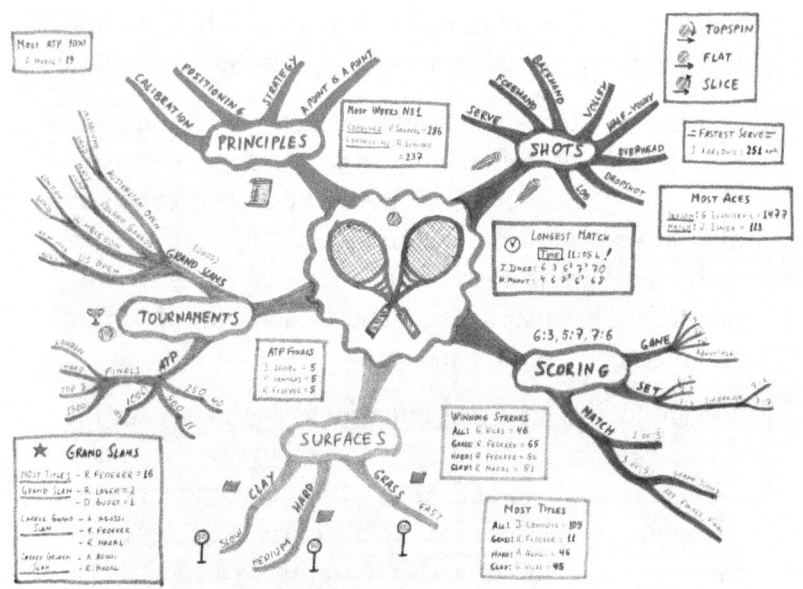

http://mindmapping.bg/mindmaps/examples/handmade/#!prettyPhoto

Story building

Andrew Williams, in his book *Brain Training: 32 Underused Techniques to Improve Memory and Critical Thinking,* says, 'You too can learn the small tweaks that yield amazingly large results in your recall. Even if you only choose one of these, you'll realize a noticeable increase in your ability to remember.'

For example, can you memorize the order of a shuffled deck of cards within an hour? This is one of the more challenging tasks given to America's most gifted children on the competition series *Child Genius*. Child prodigy Katherine, aged eleven, completed this perfectly in less than three minutes. Then she recited all fifty-two cards forward, then backwards, then correctly gave the position of random cards in the deck!

How does she do it? Katherine associates each card with unique images of people, places, animals and things and then incorporates these images into a story, connecting every card to a particular element in that story. Lisa Van Gemert, of the elite IQ society American Mensa, says that Katherine's technique is common among extraordinary children. 'You're going to be able to tell the difference between kids who use those systems and kids who just try good old-fashioned memorizing where you are reciting what you are trying to remember over and over again to keep it in your head, the same way you and I would with a phone number,' she says.

It is now well-proven that the most effective way to retain information in your brain is by linking it to existing information that's already embedded there. These memory techniques can really help. You first need to think about what it is that you learn and remember easily. Lyrics of songs? Pictures? Choreography? If you're having difficulty in memorizing something, write a catchy jingle or poem about it; else choreograph some representative dance moves; else draw an outrageous comic. Sillier stuff is easier to recall, so have fun!

When I taught Class Two arithmetic to my nephew many years ago, he said that he found the sums difficult and boring. So I closed the textbook and began telling an interactive story in which he went to the market with twenty rupees, bought some toys, games, biscuits, and so on, and asked him how much money was left after each transaction. He enjoyed the story and gave the right answers each time without using paper or pencil, but I noted his answers. Then I opened the textbook and showed how he had mentally arrived at the right answers, which thrilled him and boosted his self-confidence. Today, he is a successful businessman, a chartered accountant who avoids calculators, and finds errors in Excel sheets by just scanning them. See what a story can do!

Dale Carnegie, author of the 1936 bestseller *How to Win Friends and Influence People*, was the creator of many self-improvement courses, which have trained more than eight million people, including billionaire Warren Buffett.

In his book *Public Speaking and Influencing Men in Business*, Carnegie writes that, 'The secret of a good memory is thus the secret of forming diverse and multiple associations with every fact we care to retain.' So we need to form 'word pictures', repeat them, use them in our speech for anything we need to remember: Dates, facts, names, rules, lists, vocabulary or anything else.

The more memorable the story that you create, the easier it is to remember. Let me give you an example. To remember the names of the seven dwarfs in the fairy tale *Snow White*, you could make up the following story: I'm usually *Sleepy* when I wake up at seven in the morning, but today I was wide awake and *Grumpy* because I knew I had to visit the *Doc*. I'm normally quite *Bashful* about going, but a friend told me not to be so *Dopey*, as I had an allergy that was making me very *Sneezy*. After that I went and was given an antihistamine and was really very *Happy*.

Mnemonics

Consider the sentence, '**M**y **V**ery **E**asy **M**ethod **J**ust **S**peeds **U**p **N**aming **P**lanets'. Now consider the letter that each word starts with—M, V, E, M, J, S, U, N, P. In effect this single sentence can help you remember the names of the planets in the solar system in the right order—Mercury, Venus, Earth, Mars, Jupiter, Saturn, Uranus, Neptune and Pluto (you may decide if you wish to include Pluto or not). Consider another one: '**P**lease **E**xcuse **M**y **D**ear **A**unt **S**ally'. This mnemonic can help one memorize the order in which maths operations should be carried out: Parentheses, Exponents, Multiply, Divide, Add and Subtract (the older version was BOEDMAS—**B**rackets **O**ff, **E**xponents, **D**ivide, **M**ultiply, **A**dd and **S**ubtract).

Create your own mnemonics as an effective way to remember stuff.

Songs

As part of English grammar, one needs to understand what prepositions are. As you know, prepositions are words that show the relationship between a noun or a pronoun. Schools in the US make children sing a song that is set to the tune of *Yankee Doodle*.

Yankee Doodle went to town
A-riding on a pony
Stuck a feather in his cap
And called it macaroni

Instead of those lyrics, we recite the following ones in *The Preposition Song*:

Aboard, about, above, across
Against, along, around
Amid, among, after, at
Except, for, during, down

Behind, below, beneath, beside
Between, before, beyond
By, in, from, off, on, over, of
Until, unto, upon

Under, underneath, since, up
Like, near, past, throughout, through
With, within, without, outside
Toward, inside, into, to

Flash cards

Flash cards are a superb way of helping you memorize. All you need is stacks of index cards on which you can write words, historical dates, definitions, formulae, chemical names … pretty much anything that you need to remember. The reason that they work so well is because you end up repeatedly quizzing yourself.

These days you can download computer programs that eliminate the space and cost of index cards. For example, you could use a website called quizlet.com to create flash cards. Then you can use any of the flash card apps available for your smart phone (quizlet.com also has a mobile app) and download not only your own flash cards but also those created by others.

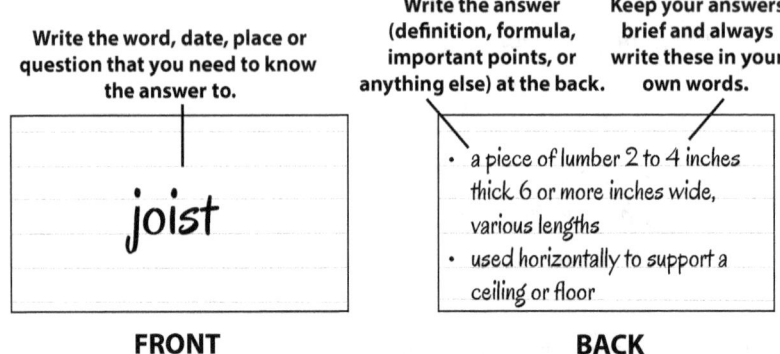

Alternatively, you can make your own cards by using a plain piece of paper folded in half (like a small greeting card). On the cover of each folding card is your question; the answer is inside the folded card. Keep quizzing yourself until you are confidently able to correctly answer all the questions in random order. It is said that repetition is the mother of skill. Remember that.

Active flash cards

What's the difference between 'flash cards' and 'active flash cards', I can hear you asking. Well, instead of simply writing a word on one side of the flash card and the definition or answer on the other, if you were to draw a unique and appropriate little picture or diagram next to the answer on the reverse, your card would now be an active flash card. The pictures or diagrams are memory aids which make your learning *active,* by which you recall the material more easily.

Pop quiz

This is a game that you can play with your friends. My father often used this method to make me memorize my multiplication tables. During any random part of the day (including at meals or in the middle of a conversation), he would suddenly ask, say, 'What is 9 × 13?' This system forces you to remain on your toes and to develop the ability to remember the information in almost *any* situation. Most importantly, it is random. You will recall that reciting the multiplication table of, say, 13, was far easier than reciting one random multiple of 13. This is because your brain had often memorized the multiples in a given order, say 13, 26, 39, 52, 65 and so on. The pop quiz method forces your brain to memorize randomly rather than sequentially.

Leitner System

The Leitner system is a popular method of learning using flash cards. Formulated by the German science journalist Sebastian Leitner in the 1970s, it involves

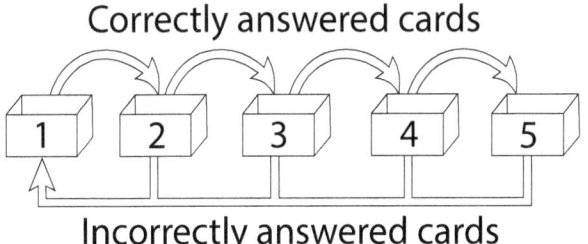

placing flash cards with correctly answered questions into later boxes and incorrectly answered flash cards into earlier boxes. In effect, the wrongly answered questions present themselves more frequently, thus forcing one to more frequently review the material that one doesn't know well enough.

Forgetting

All of us have gone through situations where we attempted to cram a set of historical dates and kept forgetting one or more of them. Don't worry. Latest research on the subject shows that forgetting is actually good. When your brain has to recall an almost obliterated memory, it has to work exceptionally hard. The result is that the dendrites dealing with that particular nugget of information become even thicker. In effect, the act of forgetting and then recalling results in a substantially improved recall.

Sleep over it

This is one little trick that very few people talk about. When getting ready to sleep, just review your summarized notes (for not more than five minutes) right before slipping into slumber. It is a well-established scientific fact that the brain strengthens new memories during sleep. Thus you are increasing the odds that you will remember whatever it is that you reviewed just before dozing off.

Understand the type of learner you are

It is important to understand that not everyone learns in exactly the same way. It has been shown that there are three basic categories of learners—visual learners, auditory learners and kinaesthetic learners. Visual learners absorb information from written words, diagrams or videos. Auditory learners are those who absorb information best from hearing or listening. Finally, kinaesthetic learners are those who need to 'do' to learn by experiencing or moving. The problem is that our education system is oriented around visual learning rather than the other two. Try and figure out what type of learner you are and develop ways to leverage that particular sense.

Audio recall

Audio recording of a lecture in the absence of making handwritten notes is not recommended. In such a situation, one tends to get lazy and allows the actual learning process to be deferred to a later time. However, if you use audio recording *in addition to* making notes, then it can be a powerful tool.

Learning tends to get better 'hardwired' when we use additional senses. One option available (depending upon the rules of the educational institution) is to record lectures on a recording device or smart phone in class and to listen to them again later.

Consider the case of Ashish Goyal, a Hedge Fund Manager at Blue Crest Capital. A post-graduate in management from Narsee Monjee Institute of Management Studies, Mumbai, he worked in the treasury department of ING Vysya Bank, then studied at the Wharton Business School, where he won the Joseph P. Wharton award, given annually to a student who symbolizes 'Wharton's way of life'. After working at J. P. Morgan as a fixed-income trader for four years, he joined Blue Crest Capital, London.

'So what?' you may very well ask. Well, Ashish was diagnosed with retinitis pigmentosa when he was nine years old and steadily lost his vision till he was completely blind at age twenty-two. But this did not stop him from studying or succeeding. He has received India's National Award for the Empowerment of Persons with Disabilities in 2010 from the President of India.

Ashish stays updated and studies using the latest technology, relying on a screen reading software which reads out to him. He now hears it at about ten times the speed at which we can speak or comprehend, understands it, remembers it, and takes business decisions based on it.

Summarize as a memory tool

One terrific way to study is to write down the key points, almost like a summary, of what you have just learned. When making summaries, use different colours. It is a well-established fact that the brain remembers information far more easily when such information is associated with colour.

Colours in notes

Various research initiatives have shown that using different colours activates different regions of our brains. This helps us remember the information better. But do not use colours randomly; be consistent. Some ace students use one colour for definitions, another for charts and yet another for examples.

Senses

Let's do a little experiment. One, close your eyes. Two, imagine an utterly sour lemon on the kitchen table. Three, imagine yourself cutting it into two. Four, imagine smelling the citrus scent. Five, imagine picking up one of the halves and squeezing the juice on your tongue. You will have noticed that your mouth has begun to water and you can almost feel that you are actually undergoing the sensations. This is the powerful link between memories and senses! If you can link information to senses, your ability to recall it will be far better.

Explain it aloud

After studying your material, explain it aloud to friends or family. In fact, you could even use the opportunity to assist friends who do not understand the material adequately. The process of explaining the information out loud results in the material being reinforced.

Ever heard of the *kindergarten rule*? This particular rule says that in order to effectively study (and learn) any material, you should be able to explain it to a six-year old child. Now, quite obviously, this will not work for differential calculus or organic chemistry, but the broad principle is that you should simplify the material so that it can be clearly understood by anyone.

Diminishing value of overlearning

Let's assume that you are using flash cards to memorize stuff. You've now been able to answer all the cards without error. Is there value in continuing the process? Continuing is considered to be 'overlearning' and older teachers and institutions usually encouraged this. But a research project at the University of South Florida and UC San Diego found that diminishing returns kick in rather quickly during overlearning. In effect, once you have studied the material and can recall it without error, it's time to stop and move on to an area that needs your attention.

Draw pictures

Certain concepts can be better remembered visually. For example, the process by which a sea breeze is created. Similarly, one could represent data in tables or Venn diagrams. The same applies to maps in geography, or the nervous system in biology. Drawing such diagrams enables you to remember the information visually. Remember the saying that a picture is worth a thousand words? It's *literally* true. If you think about it, you effortlessly remember scenes of a movie without cramming, right? In fact, using such diagrams in your answer sheet at exam time could get you a few extra marks plus refresh your memory.

Image association is a trick used by all of the world's top memory contest winners, so you know if they endorse it, we should take it very seriously! Instead of thinking of words and numbers when we try to remember something, make an effort to think in visual terms. By associating what we would like to remember with images, we are much, much more likely to remember what we wish to without struggling. There's a reason why kids in kindergarten are taught A for Apple, B for Ball and C for Cat. Associating each letter with an image helps them recollect far better!

Make a study sheet

I remember asking my co-author, Ashwin Sanghi, as to how he went about selecting the best short story from among a group of stories during a recent short story writing contest. He had a very simple solution. He read all the stories on a Saturday. He then tried to recall which stories had stuck with him on Monday. These were the stories that needed to be shortlisted for a final reading. In effect, he had found a way of being able to determine what was truly memorable.

In the world of academics, we need to determine what it is that we actually need to remember. One of the best ways of doing that is by writing up study sheets (also called 'cheat sheets').

Your effort should be to condense all the information from a particular topic into a single sheet (as shown on the following page). This forces you to pick up only the most vital points. These sheets can be repeatedly reviewed in the run-up to the exams.

Metaphors

A metaphor is a figure of speech which makes an implicit, implied or hidden comparison between two things that are unrelated but share some common characteristics. For example, 'I was boiling mad' compares my angry state to a pot of boiling water. You will be surprised that metaphors are a great way to remember things. For example, in the world of computer programming, one has to understand the concepts of parameter, function and processes. Now, if one were to imagine a dull pencil as the parameter, a pencil sharpener as the function and the act of sharpening as the process, the entire concept can be far better understood and memorized.

FUNCTIONS OF SEVERAL VARIABLES	$z=f(x,y)_{2D}$, $w=f(x,y,z)_{3D}$ DOMAINS: Allowed (x,y), (x,y,z) RANGES: z's, w's
LEVEL CURVES one/down — FUNCTION OF n VARIABLES	ϵ-δ DEFINITION OF CONTINUITY
$z=f(x,y)=k=\text{CONST.}$ $z=f(x_1,x_2,\ldots,x_n) \Leftrightarrow f(\vec{x})=\vec{c}\cdot\vec{x}$	LET f BE A FUNCTION OF 2 VARIABLES DEFINED ON A DISK W/ CENTER (a,b), EXCEPT POSSIBLE @ (a,b). THEN $\lim_{(x,y)\to(a,b)} f(x,y)=L$
CONTOUR MAPS (2-D) — $\mathbb{R}^n \to \mathbb{R}$ 3 WAYS TO LOOK @ THIS FUNCTION $\vec{z}=(c_1\ldots c_n)$	IF FOR EVERY $\epsilon > 0$, THERE IS A CORRESPONDING $\delta > 0$ s.t. IF $(x,y)-L$ < ϵ whenever $0 < \sqrt{(x-a)^2+(y-b)^2} < \delta$
$w=f(x,y,z)=k=\text{CONST.}$ 1. As a Function of n real variables $(y_1, x_2,\ldots, x_n)$	
SURFACE LAYERS (3 D) 2. As a function of a single pt. variable $(x_1, \ldots, x_n)$	
3. As a function of a single vector var $\vec{x}=(x_1\ldots x_n)$	

PARTIAL DERIVATIVES	Derivatives w/ Respect to one variable while holding the other variables Constant
$z=f(x,y)$ NOTATIONS	① IF THE LIMIT AS A FUNCTION APPROACHES A POINT (a,b) ALONG TWO DIFFERENT PATHS IS NOT THE SAME, THE LIMIT DOES NOT EXIST ⊙
$f_x(x,y)=f_x=\dfrac{\partial f}{\partial x}=\dfrac{\partial f(x,y)}{\partial x}=\dfrac{\partial z}{\partial x}$ SAME HOLDS FOR FUNCTIONS OF MORE THAN TWO VARIABLES	② $f(x,y)$ IS CONTINUOUS AT (a,b) IF THE LIMIT OF (x,y) AS $(x,y)\to(a,b)$ EXISTS.
$f_y(x,y)=f_y=\dfrac{\partial f}{\partial y}=\dfrac{\partial f(x,y)}{\partial y}=\dfrac{\partial z}{\partial y}$	③ COMPOSITE FUNCTIONS OF CONTINUOUS FUNCTIONS ARE CONTINUOUS, AS ARE SUMS AND PRODUCTS

SECOND PARTIAL DERIVATIVES	CLAIRAUT'S THEOREM	EQUATIONS OF TANGENT PLANES TO SURFACES
$f_{xx}=\dfrac{\partial}{\partial x}\left(\dfrac{\partial f}{\partial x}\right)=\dfrac{\partial^2 f}{\partial x^2}=\dfrac{\partial^2 z}{\partial x^2}=\dfrac{\partial}{\partial x}\left(\dfrac{\partial z}{\partial x}\right)$	IF f_{xy} AND f_{yx} ARE BOTH CONTINUOUS $f_{xy}(a,b)=f_{yx}(a,b)$	$z=f(x,y)$ @ (x_0,y_0,z_0) EVALUATED ATA POINT $z-z_0=f_x(x_0,y_0)(x-x_0)+f_y(x_0,y_0)(y-y_0)$
$f_{xy}=\dfrac{\partial}{\partial y}\left(\dfrac{\partial f}{\partial x}\right)=\dfrac{\partial^2 f}{\partial y\partial x}=\dfrac{\partial^2 z}{\partial y\partial x}=\dfrac{\partial}{\partial y}\left(\dfrac{\partial z}{\partial x}\right)$		TOTAL DIFFERENTIAL $(dy=f'(x)dx$ SINGLE VALUE$)$
$f_{yx}=\dfrac{\partial}{\partial x}\left(\dfrac{\partial f}{\partial y}\right)=\dfrac{\partial^2 f}{\partial x\partial y}=\dfrac{\partial^2 z}{\partial x\partial y}=\dfrac{\partial}{\partial x}\left(\dfrac{\partial z}{\partial y}\right)$	PARTIAL DIFF. EQ'S LAPLACE'S EQUATION $\dfrac{\partial^2 u}{\partial x^2}+\dfrac{\partial^2 u}{\partial y^2}=0$ etc...	$dz=f_x(x,y)dx+f_y(x,y)dy=\dfrac{\partial z}{\partial x}dx+\dfrac{\partial z}{\partial y}dy$
$f_{yy}=\dfrac{\partial}{\partial y}\left(\dfrac{\partial f}{\partial y}\right)=\dfrac{\partial^2 f}{\partial y^2}=\dfrac{\partial^2 z}{\partial y^2}=\dfrac{\partial}{\partial y}\left(\dfrac{\partial z}{\partial y}\right)$	THE WAVE $\dfrac{\partial^2 u}{\partial t^2}=a^2\dfrac{\partial^2 u}{\partial x^2}$ EQUATION ETC...	INCREMENTS $\Delta x, \Delta y, \Delta z$ DIFFERENTIALS dx, dy, dz

THE CHAIN RULE SINGLE VARIABLE $y=f(x), x=g(t), ie z=f(g(t))$
$y'(t)=f'(g(t))\cdot g'(t); \dfrac{dy}{dt}=\dfrac{dy}{dx}\cdot\dfrac{dx}{dt}$

⊙ IF f_x AND f_y ARE CONTINUOUS $\Delta z \approx dz$ (ie change in height of Surface (Δz) ≈ change in height of the tangent plane (dz)

CASE 1 $z=f(x,y)$, $x=g(t)$, $y=h(t)$ ie $z=f(g(t),h(t))$
$\dfrac{dz}{dt}=\dfrac{\partial z}{\partial x}\dfrac{dx}{dt}+\dfrac{\partial z}{\partial y}\dfrac{dy}{dt}$ or $w/z=f$ $\dfrac{\partial z}{\partial t}=\dfrac{\partial z}{\partial x}\dfrac{dx}{dt}+\dfrac{\partial z}{\partial y}\dfrac{dy}{dt}$ SAME PARTIAL

$\Delta z=f(a+\Delta x, b+\Delta y)-f(a,b)$ THEOREM
$\Delta z=f_x(a,b)\Delta x+f_y(a,b)\Delta y+\epsilon_1\Delta x+\epsilon_2\Delta y$ when ϵ_1 and ϵ_2 are functions of Δx and Δy that Approach 0 as $(\Delta x, \Delta y)\to(0,0)$ DEF.

CASE 2 $z=f(x,y)$, $x=g(s,t)$, $y=h(s,t)$ ie $z=f(g(s,t),h(s,t))$
$\dfrac{\partial z}{\partial s}=\dfrac{\partial z}{\partial x}\dfrac{\partial x}{\partial s}+\dfrac{\partial z}{\partial y}\dfrac{\partial y}{\partial s}$ $\dfrac{\partial z}{\partial t}=\dfrac{\partial z}{\partial x}\dfrac{\partial x}{\partial t}+\dfrac{\partial z}{\partial y}\dfrac{\partial y}{\partial t}$ THINGS APPEAR TO CANCEL EVERY TIME y X,Y DON'T DO THAT

⇒ f is DIFFERENTIABLE @ (a,b) for $z=f(x,y)$

CHAIN RULE: GENERAL VERSION $u=f(x_1,\ldots,x_n)$ $x_j=g_j(t_1,\ldots,t_m)$
u is a function of $t_1\ldots t_m$ $j=1,2,\ldots,n$ $i=1,2,\ldots,m$
$\dfrac{\partial u}{\partial t_i}=\dfrac{\partial u}{\partial x_1}\dfrac{\partial x_1}{\partial t_i}+\dfrac{\partial u}{\partial x_2}\dfrac{\partial x_2}{\partial t_i}+\ldots+\dfrac{\partial u}{\partial x_n}\dfrac{\partial x_n}{\partial t_i}$ for each $i=1,2,\ldots,m$

DEPENDENCY DIAGRAMS | CASE 1,2 You can find DERIVATIVES FOR ALL THE FUNDAMENTAL INDEPENDENT VARS

IMPLICIT DIFFERENTIATION You can always solve for y and diff. ⊙ ∂x, ∂y have NO MEANING like dx and dy
$\dfrac{dy}{dx}=\dfrac{\partial F/\partial x}{\partial F/\partial y}=-\dfrac{F_x}{F_y}$ $\dfrac{\partial z}{\partial x}=\dfrac{\partial F/\partial x}{\partial F/\partial z}=-\dfrac{F_x}{F_z}$ $\dfrac{\partial z}{\partial y}=\dfrac{\partial F/\partial y}{\partial F/\partial z}=-\dfrac{F_y}{F_z}$

THE GRADIENT VECTOR $z=f(x,y)$ AT A POINT
$\nabla f(x,y)=\left(\dfrac{\partial f}{\partial x}(x,y), \dfrac{\partial f}{\partial y}(x,y)\right)=(f_x, f_y)=\left(\dfrac{\partial z}{\partial x}, \dfrac{\partial z}{\partial y}\right)$

$F(x,y)=0$ $y=f(x), F(x,f(x))\equiv 0$ $F(x,y,z)=0$ $z=f(x,y)$, $F(x,y,f(x,y))\equiv 0$

DIRECTIONAL DERIVATIVES $D_{\vec{u}}f$, $\vec{u}=(a,b)$

TANGENT PLANE TO A LEVEL SURFACE $\nabla f \perp$ to Tan. Vector
$F_x(x-x_0)+F_y(y-y_0)+F_z(z-z_0)=0$ PT. EVALUATING (x_0,y_0,z_0) $\nabla f\cdot \vec{r}'(t)=0$

$D_{\vec{u}}f(x,y)=f_x(x,y)a+f_y(x,y)b$ SAME FOR 3 VARIABLES
$D_{\vec{u}}f(x,y)=\nabla f(x,y)\cdot\vec{u}$

NORMAL LINE TO A LEVEL SURFACE $\dfrac{x-x_0}{F_x}=\dfrac{y-y_0}{F_y}=\dfrac{z-z_0}{F_z}$ ALL $@(x_0,y_0,z_0)$

SPECIAL CASE $z=f(x,y)$ $F(x,y,z)=f(x,y)-z=0$ LEVEL SURFACE W/ K=0 OLD DEFINITION
THEN $F_z=-1$, $\nabla f=(f_x, f_y, -1)$ and TAN PLANE SHOWN BY $z-z_0=f_x(x-x_0)+f_y(y-y_0)$

$D_{\vec{u}}f=\nabla f\cdot \vec{u}=|\nabla f||\vec{u}|\cos\theta=|\nabla f|\cos\theta$ ($|\vec{u}|=1=\cos 0$)

⊙ THE GRADIENT VECTOR POINTS IN THE DIRECTION OF HIGHEST ASCENT OR DESCENT (ON A SURFACE)

MAXIMUM AND MINIMUM VALUES $z=f(x,y)$
$f_x(a,b)=0$ $f_y(a,b)=0$ $Df(a,b)=(0,0)=\vec{0}$ NECESSARY BUT NOT SUFFICIENT TO GUARANTEE A MAX. OR MIN.

⊙ THE GRADIENT VECTOR IS ORTHOGONAL TO THE LEVEL CURVES OF A SURFACE

① Set $f_x=f_y=0$ Solve for critical pts. (Always check $(0,0)$ if f goes thru origin)
THEN APPLY THE 2ND DERIVATIVE TEST. FIND $f_{xx}, f_{yy}, f_{xy}=f_{yx}$

⊙ ∇f HAS AS MANY COMPONENTS AS f HAS INDEPENDENT VARIABLES. N (f_x, f_y, f_z)

$D=\begin{vmatrix} f_{xx} & f_{xy} \\ f_{yx} & f_{yy} \end{vmatrix}=f_{xx}f_{yy}-(f_{xy})^2$ • D>0, $f_{xx}>0$ LOCAL MIN. • D>0, $f_{xx}<0$ LOCAL MAX • D<0 SADDLE PT. D=0 WE DON'T KNOW NOTHING

⊙ To FIND THE NORMAL (AND LATER TANGENT PLANE) TO A SURFACE, LET THAT SURFACE BE THE LEVEL SET OF SOME HIGHER DIMENSIONAL FUNCTION. THEN THE GRADIENT OF THE HIGHER D FUNCTION IS $\perp$ TO YOUR SURFACE

FINDING ABSOLUTE MAX. AND MINS FOR f ON A CLOSED BOUNDED SET
1. Find values of f at the critical points of find
2. Find the extreme values of f on the boundary of D
3. The largest value from 1,2. Is the ABS. MX. the smallest is the ABS.L

ex: $\nabla f \vec{n}$ to $x^2+y^2+z^2=1$ Let $w=x^2+y^2+z^2-1$
$x^2+y^2+z^2=1$ is THE LEVEL SET W=0
So $\nabla w=(2x, 2y, 2z)$ is A NORMAL VECTOR TO THE 3-D SPHERE $x^2+y^2+z^2=1$

MAXIMIZING AND MINIMIZING 'SETS' on a function of two Variables of the form $z=f(x,y)$ and then Do the Usual Routine

Chunking

Recent research has shown that people who are given the task of memorizing a list of thirty words will remember some words from the beginning and others from the end, but very few words from the middle of the list. What is at play is the combination of two effects: Primacy and recency.

Primacy is the effect by which words from the beginning of the list are easier to recall than words lower down. Recency is the effect by which words encountered most recently (usually at the bottom of the list) are far easier to recall.

What is the solution? It's called *chunking*. For example, a thirty-word list could be broken down into three lists of ten words each. Now study these three chunks independently. Your advantage? Each list has a beginning and an end, hence you have increased the probability of remembering those words.

Clustering

Imagine that you are given a list of words to remember. For example, here's a list of twenty-five words that you need to memorize:

Lion, Paper, Jazz, Car, Sandwich, Elephant, Pen, Rock, Airplane, Pizza, Buffalo, Clips, Pop, Train, Soup, Deer, Ink, Classical, Bus, Salad, Monkey, Eraser, Blues, Ship, Cookie.

If you run through the list and then put the list away to see which words you can recall, you should be able to recall around half. But imagine if you could 'cluster' or 'group' these words into categories. For example:

Animals: Lion, Elephant, Buffalo, Deer, Monkey
Stationery: Paper, Pen, Clips, Ink, Eraser
Music: Jazz, Rock, Pop, Classical, Blues
Transport: Car, Airplane, Train, Bus, Ship
Food: Sandwich, Pizza, Soup, Salad, Cookie

Chances are that you will be able to easily memorize the entire list.

Before we proceed further …

The forgetting curve reinforces the need to review material within twenty-four hours of learning it for the first time. You should consider creating mind maps to remember important concepts and building stories, songs and metaphors for better recall. Mnemonics, audio recall, chunking, study sheets, pictures, flash cards (using the Leitner system), active flash cards, pop quizzes and explaining aloud are great ways to master information. If you forget something and eventually struggle till you get the answer, it helps reinforce the material. Sleeping over your key points helps hardwire or embed the information.

STEP 7: PRACTICE MAKES PERFECT

Here's a story to ponder over:

A big game hunter saw a large Bengal tiger as he walked through the forest. Given that the tiger was just a short distance away, the hunter chanced a quick shot but missed. In the meantime, the tiger leaped towards the hunter, but overshot him and landed elsewhere. It was a lucky break for the hunter.

The much-relieved hunter made his way back to camp, but his poor aim was nagging him. So the next day, he went to the thicket bordering the camp in order to practise his target shooting at short range.

He stopped when he heard a rustling noise in the bushes nearby. He warily took a few steps towards the rustling sound and was dumbfounded by the sight that he saw.

The very same tiger was practising how to take short leaps so that he would not mess up the next time!

Jokes apart, the truth is that practice is critical for everyone. Working on model papers (with the same time limit as the actual examination) is an important part of preparation. Treating these model papers as actual exams gives you the ability to write the actual exam within the time limit, plan your answering strategy, and improve your confidence and knowledge level.

Model tests give you the mindset to test your knowledge, mimic actual exams, pace yourself, and plan the right strategy to tackle each subject. In fact, repeatedly attempting model papers is an important strategy of various tutorials which help students succeed in various entrance exams. The confidence gained by repeatedly attempting model papers wipes out any tension you may get while actually writing the actual exams. If you are unable to complete any question in a model paper during your mock exam, underline it and attack it immediately after with no delay.

The American writer and speaker, Earl Nightingale, had famously said, 'If a person will spend one hour a day on the same subject for five years, that person will be an expert on that subject.'

In similar vein, the journalist Malcolm Gladwell took that a step further with his 10,000-Hour Rule. In 2008, Gladwell published his *New York Times* bestseller, *Outliers*. The book considered a number of 'outliers', people who were incredibly proficient in certain subjects or skills. Gladwell found that the common factor across these individuals was the amount of time that they had devoted to practising within that specific area. He found that anyone could become an expert at anything by devoting 10,000 hours to it—or ninety minutes per day over twenty years!

The same principle applies to practice exams. The important fact to note is that an article in *Science* magazine demonstrated that students who tested themselves after studying a topic retained an incredible 50 per cent more of the material a week later than students who did not test themselves. Always merge practice tests into your study routine. Helen Keller had said, 'There are no shortcuts to any place worth going.' This could easily apply to practice.

It is said that Eklavya was an entirely self-taught archer inspired by a statue of Arjuna's guru, Dronacharya. In effect, he became a master simply through years of practice!

'Do' vs. 'Read' Subjects

It was the great Confucius who said, 'I hear and I forget. I see and I remember. I do and I understand.' So remember this: Subjects are of two types—'Do' and 'Read'. Subjects such as maths or physics are 'do' subjects. One needs to solve questions in order to become proficient with the syllabus. On the other hand, subjects like languages or social sciences are 'read' subjects. Reading, re-reading and recalling is what works for such subjects. It is important not to try using one strategy for the other.

Return to last year's books

Sometimes you may find that in subjects like maths or physics, you are unable to grasp the very fundamentals of a problem. It's an indication that you may have missed out on something in your covered syllabus. It's always a good idea to retain the textbooks of the last two years. During holidays or vacations, you should consider revisiting them in order to revise those theories and concepts that may be related to material being taught in the current year.

Practice material

The questions and problems that you use to practise the concepts could be the problems given in class, provided in your textbook, previous years' questions that may have been published or shared, as well as material available in study guides or coaching class handouts. As you attempt to solve more and more problems, you will find that the techniques become second nature and instinctive.

'Doing' requires understanding

Just cramming for exams without understanding or knowing how the knowledge is useful is counter-productive. Understanding a lesson and trying to explain it in your own words gives immense benefits.

The effort embeds the information in your mind and you get deeper insight as your knowledge and mastery over the subject improves. The American teacher, Craig McCraw, rightly observed, 'The more you understand, the less you have to remember.'

When you are writing project reports for your graduation and post-graduation, and theses for Ph.D.s, you have to take information from various sources, understand it, collate it as needed, derive observations and conclusions and prepare your final reports. Unless you have understood the inputs and expressed them error-free in your own words, it is assumed you are just copying, and your reports will be rejected for plagiarism. So it is always better to make a habit of digesting your lessons and refining them in your own words.

Our brains work like filing cabinets, indexing our daily activities and countless pieces of information for retrieval. But why are some experiences and information remembered, not others? We forget mainly because there is no association, link or hook to recall this new information. So while studying, read slowly, understand the lesson, ruminate on it, ask if you have understood it, if it makes sense, how it fits with earlier knowledge, as well as look for practical examples. With this habit, you will definitely become a fast learner, will retain your lessons, and learn to apply them in future.

There is a fundamental difference between hearing and listening; between seeing and observing; and between eating and digesting. That's the difference between cramming and understanding. When you do short-term cramming for exams, you load the information in your short-term memory, reproduce it to the best of your memory in the answer paper and then forget it.

This is not to suggest that memorizing or getting good marks from such memorizing is bad. The problem lies in 'mugging' without understanding. If you understand and then memorize, it would be impossible to get poor marks.

Use the net … but judiciously

Count your blessings. Today's students are extremely lucky because they are given extremely well-written textbooks, have access to online study materials which explain lessons with pictures and animations, online educational apps and lessons, and tutorials which enable them to have mock tests.

Today's student lives in an age where almost every key subject has already been discussed on the Internet and posted about. Almost anything and everything you could want can be found on the net. Searching for an appropriate video that explains the material that you need to study is a good idea.

The documentaries or lessons on the net are a great way of compressing an entire story (say, in history) or an entire topic (say, the Big Bang in physics) into a significantly shortened timeframe. Watching such documentaries enables you to visualize some of the concepts that your textbook may be unable to reveal. But YouTube or Vimeo or any of the other streaming websites should be used as additional, not primary, resources. Also, beware of getting distracted by other stuff on the Internet leading to black holes where your time gets burnt!

Contextual learning helps

So here's a joke: A physics teacher is telling her students, 'Isaac Newton was sitting under a tree when an apple fell on his head and he discovered gravity. Isn't that wonderful?' One of the kids gets up and says, 'Yes ma'am. And if he had been sitting in class all day looking at textbooks like us, he wouldn't have discovered anything.'

Some people learn by reading, listening or seeing. But there are also those who learn by doing. This is known as contextual learning—relating the subject matter to real world situations. Now, obviously there are limitations to this form of studying, because you simply cannot attempt to cover your entire exam syllabus through practical examples. But there are ways that you can indeed apply this to your learning.

Maths is a subject that lends itself to contextual learning. Almost every maths problem is based on a real-world situation and contextual learners can easily find ways to set up examples for themselves.

Holistic learning

Have you heard the story in which six blind men were asked to describe an elephant just by touching different parts of the animal's body?

One of them feels a leg and says the elephant is like a pillar. The second man feels the tail and says the elephant is like a rope. The third feels the trunk and describes the elephant as a huge snake. The fourth feels an ear and describes the elephant as a hand-held fan. The fifth feels the animal's belly and says that the elephant is like a wall. The sixth feels a tusk and describes the elephant as a curved and pointed rod.

Six men touch the same animal, yet provide totally different descriptions. Why? Because they cannot experience the elephant in totality. Experiencing the subject in totality is what holistic learning is about. Holistic learning is all about understanding the concepts at a significantly deeper level than usual. Remember one thing though. You cannot attempt holistic learning the night before the exam. This should be done weeks in advance.

The moot point is: You should attempt to learn holistically by interlinking ideas and information. Individual elements—formulae, theorems, dates or names—are like little pieces of a giant jigsaw puzzle. Instead of only learning each item as individual and distinct, your aim should be to consciously interlink this to anything else that strikes you as being similar. Think of the concept as a web in which each element is connected to many others. Let me give you just one example.

In the world of physics, we have two opposite concepts: Acceleration and deceleration. In the former, the speed of an object increases over time whereas in the latter, it reduces over time. The effect of acceleration and deceleration can be depicted in graphs as follows:

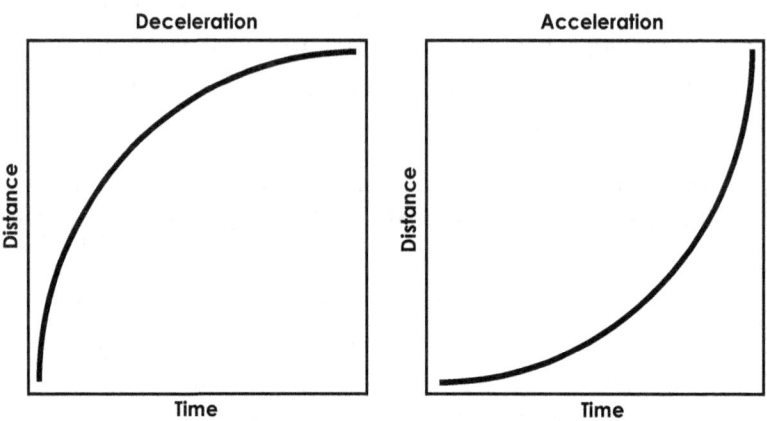

Now, the world of economics has a theory: The Law of Diminishing Marginal Utility. It states that as a person increases consumption of a product, there is a decline in the 'marginal utility' that person derives from consuming each additional unit of that product.

Another concept is that of compound interest, in which the growth of an initial investment speeds up with time owing to the compounding effect. Both these concepts can be graphically represented as:

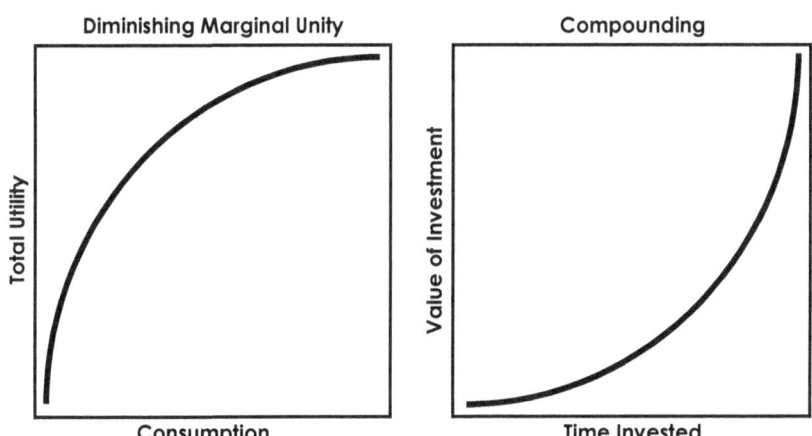

Do you see the similarities? In effect, if one understands the broad principles in one discipline, say, physics, one finds it easier to understand similar principles in economics. This is the essence of holistic learning.

Before we proceed further …

One must distinguish between 'do' and 'read' subjects and apply the principle of practice to all 'do' subjects. Doing necessarily involves understanding the material rather than simply cramming. Take advantage of practice questions and exams from as many sources as possible. If you find yourself struggling, go back to the previous year's material to check if some of your foundation blocks need brushing up. Take advantage of YouTube and other resources to find videos or presentations that explain the subject in an easy-to-learn way. Find ways to apply your learning to the real world. This is called contextual learning. Attempt to interlink ideas, information and concepts between disciplines, thus leveraging the holistic learning ability of the human brain.

STEP 8: BUILD YOUR NETWORK

Have you heard the fable about Tommy the lion?

Tommy was separated as a cub from his pride and ended up following a flock of sheep. Brought up among sheep, he naturally thought of himself only as a sheep.

One day, Tommy heard the roar of a lion. Along with the rest of the flock, he too ran for cover. The roaring lion was amazed to see Tommy, a fully-grown lion, behaving almost completely like a sheep.

He managed to separate Tommy from the flock and explained that Tommy wasn't a sheep but a lion, but Tommy refused to believe it. After all, he had spent most of his life among sheep.

The lion eventually led Tommy to a pond and showed him that they looked almost identical in the reflection. That's when the truth struck Tommy. He had been behaving like a sheep simply because he had been part of the flock.

You must have heard the proverb that a man is known by the company he keeps. Another one says that birds of a feather flock together. So how are these proverbs applicable here? When you are in a group, you tend to behave in a similar manner, either because you are following the leader, or due to peer pressure.

Do you know the difference between a piece of iron and a magnet? Both have the same atomic structure; each and every iron atom is a magnet with a north and a south pole. In an ordinary piece of iron, these atoms are arranged randomly, with each north pole being neutralized by an adjacent south pole and vice versa. The effect is that the atoms form closed loops and the piece does not exhibit magnetic properties. When attached to, or placed near, a permanent magnet or electromagnet, the same piece of soft iron behaves like a magnet but loses that property when the magnet is removed. And a permanent magnet gets demagnetized when heated or stuck sharply. So also, being in the company of bright and successful persons can align your thought processes and habits in the right direction. The right company will raise you to new heights; the wrong company will drag you to failure.

Classmates

If your group of friends is always discussing movies, games or TV shows, you are unlikely to concentrate on your studies in their presence. So if you wish to excel in your studies and get excellent marks, you should change your orbit and move with studious classmates. Group study with classmates whose level of preparation is approximately equal to yours can be helpful. You can discuss lessons, clarify each other's doubts, collect earlier question papers and analyze them to estimate probable questions for your class. This does not mean that you should forsake friends who are not studious. You simply need to avoid them as part of your study network.

Teachers

Another important but overlooked resource are your teachers. Most students are reluctant to seek time outside class or to ask questions inside class. Change that habit! Most teachers are happy to assist their students inside and outside of class once they are aware that the student in question is sincere.

Group study

What about group study? Just ask yourself if your group actually does study together, or if you are better off studying on your own. Possibly having a parent present during a session will give you an expert outside opinion. When you feel like slacking off, seeing others studying around you can pull you back into a disciplined routine. If each of you studies certain topics independently and then teaches the studied topic to others in the group, you actually enhance the hardwiring of that material in your brain. But this entirely depends on the group. Very often, group study can also mean lots of distractions or idle chatter.

The value of teaching others

The brain has a network of fibre pathways that contain around 100 billion neurons. When we learn anything new, new fibres, called dendrites, grow from the existing neurons. As individual dendrites grow, connections are created between them. These are called synapses. These synapses become stronger and thicker as your learning of something improves. The more the number of senses involved in learning, the thicker and stronger the synapses.

Just think about it. We tend to easily recall smells, tastes and songs. We also effortlessly recall pleasant, unpleasant, happy, unhappy and comical experiences. But this ease of recall does not apply to neutral experiences, which have no 'hooks' to easily attach to. Most of our lessons are just words in textbooks, spoken by teachers, heard and written by us. But our memory holds information in the form of pictures, sounds, smells, tastes, tactile sensations and experiences, which is the reason why remembering only words is challenging. So we need to form word-pictures or hooks so that the lessons 'stick' and are easy to recall.

Edgar Dale created a theory that was called the *Cone of Experience*. This theory was based upon a 1967 article by a Mobil Oil employee, D. G. Treichler. It was further refined by the Colorado Department of Education in 1999. In this framework, it is explained that we learn:

5 per cent of what we hear in lectures
10 per cent of what we read
20 per cent of audio visual material presented
30 per cent of what is demonstrated
50 per cent of what we discuss
75 per cent of what we practice by doing
90 per cent of what we teach others

Now, please do not consider this the absolute truth. It is not. But it does drive home the point that our ability to learn is vastly improved as we involve more of our senses. And one of the best ways to learn something is to actually teach it to someone else!

This could involve you teaching your classmates or you could simply explain your learning out aloud to a family member. The mere act of explaining or teaching has an incredible effect.

Coaching classes

Let's face it. We live in an era of competitive exams. Whether it is the tenth or twelfth standard board exams such as CBSE, SSC, ICSE, HSC or entrance exams such as the IIT-JEE, CAT, MAT or the Civil Services, given the intense competition to get in, coaching classes that can give one 'an edge' have mushroomed all over the country.

I do not believe in extreme views regarding coaching classes. One extreme view holds that *all* coaching classes are money-making rackets. Another extreme view is that coaching classes are the *only* solution to scoring high marks. So what should you do? As with all issues, there are points in favour and against.

Reasons why coaching classes are a good option:

1. Most coaching institutes specialize in a particular type of competitive exam. This means that they are 'specialists' and can provide you with tips, tricks, techniques and material that may not be available to you otherwise.
2. Your coaching class becomes your one-stop shop for everything related to that upcoming exam. Usually the notes and material are perfectly drafted and are far easier to grasp than regular textbooks.
3. Coaching institutes provide their students with exceptionally well-organized study patterns. Usually they make their students spend several hours on practice tests and questions. The end result is that such students are usually very well-prepared and confident for the actual exam.
4. Coaching classes create an environment in which even lazy students have no option but to catch up.
5. Students planning on taking the Civil Services, M.B.A., Engineering or Medical entrance exams not only require preparation but also guidance and mentoring. They are often able to get this from their professors at coaching institutes.

Reasons why coaching classes are not a good option:

1. Many students end up joining coaching classes because of peer pressure or parental pressure, not because they have actually evaluated the strengths of that particular coaching class.
2. The fees charged by coaching classes are often exorbitant and are usually taken upfront. This means that if one were to leave midway, one would be financially at a loss.
3. An overabundance of institutes has resulted in intense competition among them. This leads to high-pitched advertising and marketing campaigns. Students often get swayed by freebies and claims in ads.
4. Coaching classes do not allow students to explore the subject fully on their own. They often provide tips and techniques that, in some ways, go against the very idea of organic learning.
5. Weaker students often feel pressurized when surrounded by high performers in such classes. Coaching classes simply expect all their students to be up to speed and weaker students feel cheated when they are unable to keep up.
6. Coaching classes often encourage an obsessive behaviour surrounding marks, which can have fatal consequences. There have been several instances of students committing suicide as a result of the pressure created by such an environment.

What should you do when it comes to making a decision? Here are a few pointers: Do not trust the advertisements or commercials. Also do not get influenced by freebies. Speak to students who have attended previous batches. Most institutes also offer trial classes. Attend the trial sessions to determine whether the style and approach work for you. Also focus on the ratio of successful candidates to enrolment. Most institutes simply publish the names and photographs of their top performers in their ads, but what percentage of their enrolment were toppers?

Home tutors or group tuitions

A good home tutor can help accelerate your progress tremendously, but this can also mean a substantial financial outlay. If you do consider engaging a tutor, take a few precautions:

1. Check out your tutor's experience and qualification.
2. Speak to his or her previous students.
3. Evaluate several tutors and compare the fees being charged.
4. Request for a trial session and determine whether he or she has the ability to explain the material well.
5. Ensure that your tutor gives you abundant practice tests and questions.

Before we proceed further …

Associate with like-minded studious classmates so that you are able to benefit from each others' knowledge and habits. Evaluate whether group studying works for you and use it as an effective tool if it does. Do not be shy about approaching teachers for help. Most of them are happy to oblige. You can better 'hardwire' the material into your brain by teaching other members of your group or family. Rationally and unemotionally evaluate coaching class options before you decide to take the plunge. Similar evaluation must be done for a home tutor or group tuitions.

STEP 9: SHARPEN SUPPLEMENTARY SKILLS

You will be surprised to know the number of students who lose marks in exams because of poor handwriting, silly and avoidable mistakes or because of too much time spent on a simple calculation. Many are the supplementary skills that can directly or indirectly influence the marks that you get. Let's examine some of these.

Exercise your brain

The brain is not one but three. These three brains are the reptilian brain, the limbic brain and the cortical brain.

The *reptilian brain* is thus named because it is responsible for the lowest stratum of thoughts such as hunger, breathing, fight-or-flight, etc. There is something important to be understood about the reptilian brain. If you are starving, it is the reptilian brain that will rule and your higher brain activities would be minimized.

In effect, if you are hungry, sleepy, anxious or stressed, your ability to learn is severely impeded.

The *limbic brain,* also called the middle brain, is responsible for emotions, sexuality, hormones and immunity. More importantly, it is the limbic brain in which long-term memories are stored. What is the learning that follows from this revelation? If you associate your learning with emotions, you will grasp it better.

Finally, you have the *cortical brain*, the highest and outermost layer—the cortex. This is our intelligence and manages our reasoning, logic and language.

Now, please remember that the three computers in your head work as one. When you are relaxed, the interaction and exchange between them is at a peak. But when you are stressed, the connectivity is hindered.

It is important to understand that your brain has trillions of brain cells. Just the cortical brain has around a hundred billion neurons, and each is more formidable than a supercomputer. People tend to think that these neurons determine intelligence. Nonsense! What is important to note is that each neuron has the ability to make twenty thousand connections with other neurons. These connections are called dendrites and axons.

What is the difference between dendrites and axons? The easy way to understand it: Dendrites are like the telephone cables that run between your home and the telephone exchange; axons are like long-distance fibre-optic type undersea cables.

When you memorize new stuff or learn how to solve a new puzzle, you are actually (yes, physically) creating new dendrites. It is the number of dendrites that govern your intelligence. Both Einstein and you would have the same number of neurons, but Einstein's dendrites would be far more numerous. The good news is that dendrites can grow at *any* age. The bad news is that dendrites can disappear if you aren't actively using your brain power. There is a witty proverb that says: Your mind is like a parachute; it only works when it is open.

In effect, please exercise your brain, which is like a muscle. If used regularly and properly and challenged with new skills, crossword puzzles, Rubik's cube, Sudoku, Scrabble, word games, mental calculations and memory tests, it will function and grow, rather than growing weaker with advancing age. In fact, regular and challenging mental exercises can even delay the onset of Alzheimer's disease.

If left unused or underused, the brain will atrophy and die even at a young age. So make a conscious effort to minimize your dependence on calculators, computers and laptops, which have become mental crutches, yet essential for our existence. Rather, allot time to regularly exercise your grey cells. There are also many online games of skill to test and develop your brain. In short: Use it or lose it.

Handwriting

Professors grading papers are always under time pressure. So if they come across material that is difficult to read, they often end up ignoring it entirely. Some of the primary reasons for poor handwriting are:

1. Using unsuitable writing instruments (pencil is too light, ink is smudging, using colours which are not permitted, and so on).
2. Not holding the pen or pencil between the thumb and index finger (or optionally the middle finger).
3. Writing with only fingers rather than the entire hand.
4. Holding the writing instrument too tightly or too loosely.
5. Not holding the writing instrument 25-30 per cent above the writing tip.
6. Using a writing instrument not suitable for you (in terms of weight and size).
7. Using too much of a slant while writing.
8. Not doing enough writing by hand and thus losing practice.
9. Irregularity and inconsistency in letters and their shapes.

If your handwriting is poor, spend a little time in finding the right pen or pencil that really works for you. Then go back to first grade and fill up a few sheets of paper with basic alphabets (remember cursive writing?) until you are satisfied that your writing looks clean and legible.

Mental Arithmetic

I am still baffled by the speed at which the older generation can do multiplication, division, addition and subtraction in their heads. My father and grandfather could not only recite multiplication tables of integers but also of fractions. I strongly recommend that you should build your mental arithmetic skills because you will find that you will breeze through quantitative questions of examination papers. No doubt you have to give complete workings for questions involving calculations, but you can always check using mental arithmetic. Remember also that the ability to perform mental arithmetic is most useful while writing competitive examinations in the sections on computational skills.

Language fluency

Fluency is essential in the language of instruction, just as you need to learn how to use the accelerator, brake and clutch before you learn to drive a car. If you find it difficult to follow lessons because your skills are inadequate in the language of instruction, improve your language skills so that you are able to understand, think, and even dream in that language. Understanding a lesson and trying to explain it in your own words is immensely beneficial.

How can you improve your skills in the language of instruction? Let's assume that the medium of instruction is English. First decide which version you want to learn. Most Indians pronounce and write English in the British style, so that would be a safe choice. Naturally, you would begin with your textbooks and try to understand them. Use a dictionary for learning the meanings and pronunciation of unfamiliar words. Observe the sentence construction, word usage, punctuation and grammar.

Make reading any leading English newspaper a habit. Read slowly at first, then your speed will pick up as your skill improves. Conversation with parents, teachers and companions who are more fluent is most helpful. You could always hear the English news on any leading news channel and start emulating them. Of course, there is no substitute for good books and I truly believe that education should not be limited to textbooks. The same techniques can be applied to increase your fluency and expertise in any language.

Educated Indians have a unique advantage over almost every other nationality as they can read, write and speak at least two languages. Very few Indians can say their mother tongue is English, but there are more English-speaking Indians than any other nationality. The fact that English is ubiquitous in India gives Indians a huge global advantage. So how does this knowledge of English help in getting better marks? Study materials on all subjects are definitely available in English, so knowing the language is surely an advantage.

But there's more: A study by Georgetown University Medical Centre in Washington DC has found that people who are bilingual or multilingual have more grey matter. In the past it had been believed that children who spoke two languages were at a disadvantage because coping with two sets of vocabularies would cause delayed language development. But the new study revealed that such kids actually perform better on tasks that require attention and short-term memory. So there you have it. It is in your interest to know more than one language.

Many of us have had the good fortune of being exposed to English from a very young age and so we do not need to learn it afresh when the medium of instruction is English, and we find it fairly easy to follow the lessons. Many Indians are more comfortable communicating and thinking in English than in their mother tongues. But those of us who are weak in English and studying in English medium need to learn the language quickly and adequately. Even those not currently studying in English medium are advised to improve their fluency, as English is the most common international language for communication.

Another advantage of being multilingual is that you can practise explaining your lessons in your mother tongue (or in a different language) while discussing with your parents or friends. This will help you remember the lessons even better and increase your mastery over both (or all) the languages that you have used.

Word power

Word power plays an important role when it comes to subjects such as English or history. Frankly, the only real way that you can boost your vocabulary is by reading more. Not just your textbooks, but also books outside your syllabus. This includes both non-fiction and fiction. While this may not be something that you can do every day, you can certainly set reading targets for yourself during holidays and vacations. If you have no time to read, there are books that can enable you to enhance your vocabulary and language skills considerably. One example is *Word Power Made Easy* by Norman Lewis. Another example of such a book is *Word Up!* by Marcia Riefer Johnston. As stated earlier, you should also make it a habit to read the newspaper each day and if you come across words that you do not understand, you should make a note of them and then look them up in the dictionary. Over a period of time, you will find that your reading, comprehension and writing skills have improved.

Drawing

Drawing diagrams or representing material visually is a way of showing the examiner that you know your stuff. In fact, even if a diagram is not asked for and you believe that the diagram better explains the answer, it's a good idea to incorporate it (depending on time allocation). Neat and clean diagrams that are clearly labelled will indeed fetch you marks. Always use a pencil initially to make the diagram so that you have the option of using an eraser before it is final. Then, depending upon the specific rules of the exam, you may choose to leave it in pencil or you may run your pen over it to ink it. In subjects such as biology or geography, the diagrams should be practised in advance at the learning stage itself.

General knowledge

In some subjects, you may be asked to relate past events to a current one; or compare a historical figure to a current one. In such instances, your general knowledge—information that you have absorbed outside of your syllabus can help. You cannot prepare for general knowledge in the way that you study for geography. What you *can* do is to stay updated with the news. Reading non-fiction can also help. But all of these suggestions have to be implemented over a substantially long period of time. Besides this, you can also accelerate the process by picking up general knowledge guides that are published for the Civil Service exams.

> **Before we proceed further ...**
>
> You can ensure that you do not lose marks by building up supplementary skills. These include improving your handwriting, working on your mental arithmetic, practising your drawings and diagrams, building you language fluency, strengthening your vocabulary and brushing up on your general knowledge. Most importantly, keep your brain engaged in mental exercises so that it remains in peak form.

STEP 10: MANAGE YOUR ENVIRONMENT

It is important to find a quiet place to study. More importantly, it should be free of distractions. For example, if your home is always buzzing with family members, then study in your school or college library. If you get distracted by the presence of people in public spaces, lock yourself in your room. Many students make the mistake of making one of the following locations their study space:

- The bed
- The kitchen or dining-room table
- The living-room sofa
- The coffee shop where you and your friends meet
- The college canteen

To tell you the honest truth, none of the above are likely to work. What you need is a quiet space that is free from distractions. This could be a desk in your bedroom, a quiet corner spot in the college or school library or even an empty classroom.

Organize

De-clutter your desk, arrange your books and study materials to look neat and in such a logical manner that you can find anything even with your eyes closed. You should have a pre-determined place for everything—notes, homework, extra paper, supplies, etc. It prevents you from wasting time trying to find stuff.

Create the right setting

Ensure that your study area is comfortable and conducive to undisturbed study: Adequate light, breeze, comfortable seating, study materials arranged conveniently, no distractions, instrumental music if you like it, possibly the right refreshing scents (vanilla, rose, pine, eucalyptus or others), and a water bottle nearby. If some things distract you (for example, novels, phone or magazines), let them not be visible in your study area. It has been shown that a temperature between 23 and 26 degrees celsius is ideal for your brain cells.

View

I strongly recommend that your study desk should face a wall. The reason for this is that your view is blocked and you avoid getting distracted.

Change of scenery helps

According to psychologist Robert Bjork at the University of California at Los Angeles (UCLA), one of the proven study techniques that is ignored most often is the improved retention that comes from change of scenery. If you've been inside your 'organized environment' and find that you are slowing down, simply stand, go to another room or sit in the park.

Distractions

Distractions are of two types—external and internal. External distractions could include a chair that isn't comfortable, wrong temperature setting of the room, or noise from the street. In addition, we live in a connected world and our computers, tablets and phones are perpetually beeping or flashing to indicate the arrival of a new alert or message. Make it a rule to silence your phone and place it some distance away from where you are studying. Switch off your computer. In case you need it for revision, then block all distracting websites or social media apps temporarily. Research at UCLA has shown that such distractions actually do weaken your understanding capability as well as memorization. Websites like selfcontrolapp.com will allow you to cut out electronic distractions for a pre-set time interval. Internal distractions, on the other hand, are more difficult to handle. For example, if you are sleep-deprived, are in a bad relationship, suffering from bad health or plagued with financial worries, these distractions can wreak havoc on your studying.

Maintain lists

We often end up intruding on our study time because routine tasks suddenly pop into our heads. It could be a birthday, a chore, or a family event. Get into the habit of maintaining a 'to-do' list for all such tasks. What does this have to do with studying? Well, if you write these things down, you don't end up taxing your brain to remember such mundane stuff. The mere act of maintaining such a list prevents these issues from distracting you while studying.

Music

If you are using music to simply block out the noise around you, get some simple ear plugs that can reduce auditory distractions. They work wonders.

Some students prefer studying without music, while others prefer music while they study. Music can be helpful in calming you down or elevating your mood, so there is no harm in using it as a study aid. If you do need music to help you study, find something that will soothe or calm you, but under no circumstances should it distract you. Some students use instrumental music so that the words do not distract them, whereas others are fine with the words too. Slower tempo music, it is believed, relaxes the human mind and thus puts the brain into a better learning condition.

There is no right or wrong answer to this issue. You decide under what conditions you learn best. Keep in mind though that listening to the radio or television is not a good idea. The ads and the segment breaks by RJs can be rather distracting.

It was music that boosted Thomas Jefferson's efforts in writing the American Declaration of Independence. Whenever he was stuck for words, he would play his violin. Albert Einstein was a terrible student in school and had to be pulled out. Luckily, his mother introduced him to the violin, and consequently to the music of Mozart and Bach. It is indeed possible that music played a part in helping Einstein attain the dizzying heights that he did.

It is now found that western classical music from the baroque period allows the body's heartbeat and pulse rate to synchronize to the beat of the music. For example, baroque music with a rhythm of 60 beats per minute activates both the left and right brains. The simultaneous activation of both hemispheres seems to maximize learning and retention. According to The Centre for New Discoveries in Learning, learning potential can be increased a minimum of five times by using this 60 beats per minute music. Similarly, some forms of Indian classical music and Japanese meditative music also work wonders.

Before we proceed further ...

Choose your study location wisely so that you have minimal distractions. Organize your desk so that you know where everything is located. Make sure that you have everything near at hand, including a snack or a bottle of water. Do not hesitate to change your study location if you find that your concentration is dipping. Learn how to manage both external and internal distractions (including limiting the view). Use music if it works for you, but be careful in choosing music that helps you to study. Maintain task lists to avoid brain clutter.

STEP 11: MANAGE BODY AND MIND

There are several states of mind and each results in a different type of brain wave. These are: beta waves, theta waves, delta waves, alpha waves and gamma waves.

Beta waves are the electrical impulses that we associate with our ordinary waking lives—talking, walking or getting through chores. Theta waves are the impulses associated with nodding off. Delta waves are the waves that are generated during deep sleep and are the slowest of the impulses. Alpha waves are generated when we are fully awake but very relaxed. Gamma waves are the high-frequency impulses that are ideal for recall, attentiveness and studying.

Surprisingly enough, research at the University of Wisconsin has shown that one of the best ways to produce gamma waves is by meditating, Zen meditation in particular. What's the point, you may ask. Well, your body and mind have to be perfectly tuned to maximize learning. So those who think that they can have a telephone conversation while reading a chapter from the textbook need to revise their strategy.

Stress kills learning

There is a very good reason why you should not do last-minute cramming. Researchers at University of California at Irvine found that just a few hours of stress can activate hormones that release corticotropin, which disrupts the process involved in creating and registering memories. Study breaks, meditation and exercise can help you lower your corticotropin levels and thus improve your learning, but remember that last-minute studying is accompanied by stress.

Sleep and recharge

Staying up all night to study is a very risky proposition. Research from the University of Notre Dame has clearly indicated that the best way to remember information that has been memorized is to actually sleep after the process of memorization. It almost 'hardwires' the material into your brain. In the Notre Dame study, two random groups of students were observed: First, those who studied at 9 a.m. and then carried on with their normal day; second, those who studied at 9 p.m. and then went to sleep. Both groups were tested twice. Once after twelve hours and once after twenty-four hours (to ensure that both groups had had a full night's sleep). The ones who slept soon after studying were the ones who scored consistently higher.

Ideally, you should sleep at the same time every night in a room that is without disturbance. Your last meal, taken three or more hours before you go to bed, should not be too heavy or oily. Totally avoid the television, Internet, video games and other distractions just before going to sleep. But take care to avoid oversleeping. Too much sleep can make you lazy and burn up time which can be employed for useful activities.

How much sleep is too much sleep? There is no clear reply; it depends on your activity level, habits, age, health, needs, etc. But six hours is generally considered the bare minimum. Also remember that power naps (not over thirty minutes) in the middle of the day, again with relaxation techniques and deep breathing, can compensate for one to two hours of sleep reduction at night.

Maintain healthy relationships

Healthy relationships play an important role in getting your endocrine system to release the right mix of hormones. The neurons inside you respond to these hormones, thus making you even more productive. Secure and happy relationships are conducive to better learning. Remember that concentrating on your studies can become next to impossible if one or more of your relationships with family or friends are in trouble.

Exercise

Mens sana in corpore sano is a Latin phrase that means 'a sound mind in a sound body'. The benefits of exercise on the brain are many and well-documented. You can also give your studying a boost by breaking a sweat shortly before you study. According to Dr. Douglas B. McKeag of the Indiana University Medical Center, exercise gets blood flowing to your brain more evenly and makes you more alert and more able to learn. Aerobic exercise is very good for long and short term memory in addition to being good for your health. Cardiovascular exercises like running, swimming, riding a pedal bicycle or using a rowing machine are great choices. They increase your Basal Metabolic Rate by which you burn more calories for longer and also improve the volume of your entorhinal cortex, an area of the brain responsible for memory. Walking or exercising with a like-minded companion is still better with some friendly competition. If you are not very athletic, you can start with walking, build up speed, then upgrade to more strenuous exercises.

Snack smart

If you are the sort of student who gets hungry while studying, keep a few snacks by your side when you begin studying so that you do not waste time going to search for a snack during your study session. Keeping it just out of arm's reach may prevent you from frequent gorging.

Snack sensibly by eating healthy and nutritious foods instead of stuff that is loaded with sugar or fat. Snacks such as fruit, nuts and vegetables are good options. If you have a sweet tooth, dark chocolate also is an option, as is *chikki*, which contains nuts and unprocessed sugar. It has been shown that fatty foods and processed sugar slow down learning.

Avoid snacks such as instant noodles, chips and candy because they will give you a temporary rush and bring you down equally quickly. Drink water so as to remain hydrated, but if you drink too much, you will end up taking too many rest room breaks.

Have tea if you need a caffeine boost. Avoid energy drinks and sodas because the sugar in them can make you crash. If coffee or tea works for you, avoid the sugar.

Omega-3 fatty acids, found in certain types of fish, nuts and olive oil, are said to have brain-boosting capabilities. Another study discovered that consuming a combination of omega-3 and omega-6 fatty acids before a test actually lowered exam anxiety.

Your brain is 70 per cent water, so keep yourself hydrated. Many of us are actually dehydrated and we do not realize it. Please also remember that digestion uses a significant amount of energy which is delivered by blood circulation (meaning less blood is available for other functions during digestion). Eating light before a study session or a test can prevent you from feeling groggy.

Brain rhythm

Each one of us is made differently. We have individual 'peak periods' when we are most alert. For some, this is in the early hours of the morning while for others it is in the stillness of the night. Try to observe those times of the day when you are more alert. If you are not sure, try various times of the day. In effect, attempt to find out when you are more 'tuned in' and plan your study timings accordingly.

Talk to your family and tell them you need their positivity

Let me tell you a small story.

One day Thomas Edison came home from school and handed an envelope to his mother. He told her, 'My teacher gave this letter to me and asked me to only give it to my mother.' His mother's eyes were tearful as she read the letter out loud to her child. She read out, 'Your son is a genius. This school is too small for him and doesn't have enough good teachers for training him. Please teach him yourself.' Thus began Edison's home schooling. After many, many years, Edison's mother died and by then, he was considered one of the greatest inventors of the century. One day he was rummaging through old family things and he saw an envelope in the corner of a drawer in a desk. He took it and opened it to reveal the letter that he had brought back that day from school. On the letter was written, 'Your son is addled (difficult, mentally ill or utterly confused). We won't let him come to school anymore.' Edison read the letter several times and cried. Then he wrote in his diary, 'Thomas Edison was an addled child that, by a hero mother, became the genius of the century.'

What's the point? Maintaining a positive attitude is essential for learning. The responsibility for this lies not only with students, but also with their parents and friends. The problem, though, is that we can take responsibility for ourselves but not for others.

Never underestimate the power of your mind. If your peers, parents or teachers belittle you or consider you a poor student, take it as a challenge and prove them wrong! As the old proverb says: You cannot remove all the thorns in your path, but you can wear strong shoes to protect yourself! You think you can, so you can! Find ways to remain positive even in difficult times. Meditating and listening to music are great ways to do this.

Prayer and Meditation

When you meditate or pray, your brain activity moves from the right frontal cortex (the region responsible for stress) to the calm left frontal cortex. The sensation of relaxation slows down your breathing. When your breathing slows down to six breaths per minute, your breath is aligned with your heart's rhythms and this is good for cardiovascular well-being. Besides physical benefits such as decreased blood pressure, the mental benefits include better absorption, increased creativity, lowered anxiety and depression, heightened learning and memory, and elevated emotional stability. Taking out a few minutes in the day to pray can help in your studies dramatically.

Remember one thing though: Prayer or meditation cannot be a substitute for what you need to do to cover your study material. An interesting story comes to mind in this regard:

A man who had great faith in God was in his house when it was surrounded by flood water. He stood by, confident that God would come to rescue him. He refused to be rescued by his neighbours, by the fire brigade, by a boat when the flood rose, and even when a helicopter came to save him. Finally, he drowned. When he met God, he complained that He had not come to save him. God replied: 'I came four times to save you, but you refused to be saved.' Hence we have the familiar proverb: God helps only those who help themselves.

Stand up

You can get 18 per cent more oxygen to reach your brain when you are standing. This is because standing circulates more blood to the brain. I know of many students who prefer to study standing up (or even walking around).

Deep breathing

The brain is only 2 per cent of your body weight but uses 20 per cent of your oxygen intake. In effect, more oxygen equals faster learning. Compel yourself to take deep breaths during your breaks.

One of the key errors made by most people is that they breathe too fast. This also means that the breaths that they take are superficial. Breathing twenty times per minute implies that you are using less than 16 per cent of your lung capacity. What is the solution?

Simple. Slow down. Train yourself to take breaks in which you slow down to five to seven breaths per minute. You will find that your concentration increases because of the higher oxygen intake.

Trick yourself into being upbeat

In Mark Twain's *The Adventures of Tom Sawyer*, Tom's aunt orders him to paint a fence as a punishment. But Tom craftily pretends it is a great treat to be enjoyed, and tricks his friends into paying him for the 'privilege' of painting the fence. Often, this is the trickery that you need to employ within yourself in order to maintain a positive attitude.

My co-author, Ashwin Sanghi, was rejected by the publishing industry forty-seven times. I once asked him how he remained positive during those days. He replied that he put up a sign that noted the number of times that great authors such as J. K. Rowling, Stephen King and John Grisham had been rejected. Thus, when he looked at his own rejections, he no longer felt bad. It was a way of *tricking* himself into being positive, even in a bad situation. The American auto king, Henry Ford, once said, 'Whether you think you can or you think you can't, you're right.' What he meant was that if one has a positive attitude, it translates into positive actions and the reverse is also true.

Have you read *The Secret* by Rhonda Byrne? The central theme of the book is that positive thinking can create life-changing results. Positivity, which is absolutely vital in getting good marks, does not come from circumstances but from within you. It's all about your attitude. Your endocrine system responds to your positive approach in order to make you productive. Most students ask: That's all very well but how can I be positive if I have just received a poor remark or grade from my teacher? The answer is simple. Look up your old test papers and report cards. You will definitely find a few good grades and remarks within them. Put these up on the wall in your room near your desk and convince yourself that all your grades and remarks in the future will be excellent. Take every poor grade as a challenge!

Before we proceed further ...

Stress kills your learning, so figure out how to de-stress. Having adequate sleep ensures that you are fresh and capable of absorbing. It also helps cement memories. Maintaining healthy relationships is vital for effective studying. Exercise increases the oxygen supply to your brain and accelerates learning. Eat wisely so that the nutrients boost your learning capacity. Identify your peak period and use it for studying. Take your family into confidence and request them for positivity. Meditate if you can. It has been shown to help produce gamma waves that are most useful in studying. Deep breathing and intermittently standing up can also help improve concentration. Finally, you need to trick yourself into being upbeat.

STEP 12: EXAM STRATEGY

So, we're nearing the crux of this book. Long hours and days have been spent by you reading, memorizing, revising and practising ... and now exams are around the corner. Are there any best practices for dealing with exams (besides studying!)? Sure there are. Read on ...

Question patterns

Coaching centres analyze question papers of earlier years, working out possible model papers and creating mock tests. Analyzing the question papers of earlier years begins by collecting and collating question papers of the last three or more years, after verifying that the syllabus has not changed during that period. The next stage is to find the pattern of the question papers versus the syllabus. Some questions are repeated, and are therefore likely to be repeated in future also. Some topics from the syllabus only appear in short notes or carry fewer marks; you can prepare accordingly.

Based on the above analysis, possible question papers, called *model papers*, are created. These model papers follow the same format as the actual papers (same number of questions, sections, choices and allotment of marks). Model test papers are available in bookstores and online, but do ensure that you are buying only the current versions from some reputed publisher or coaching centre. But remember: You, your friends and coaching centres may be able to create possible question papers, but there is every possibility you may get other questions which you must answer.

Teacher review

If a teacher is reviewing material with your class before a test or exam, pay very close attention and make detailed notes of what is said. Usually the material covered will have a very high probability of showing up in your question paper.

Handling the exam

1. Prayer is no substitute for preparation. Practise, practise, practise (including mock-runs with earlier exam papers with time limit). This helps you overcome exam fear. Practise, especially for maths, essay-type answers and problems.
2. Some students work through the year, but do not adequately prepare on the day before the exam. This is usually not a good idea. While it is true that if you have been diligently preparing throughout

the year, you will retain at least 90 per cent in your memory, and will still get good marks, it is also true that you may end up getting nervous on exam day, which may interfere with your concentration.
3. Ensure that what you are preparing for is actually your next paper. I have seen umpteen cases of preparation done for the wrong paper.
4. Make sure that you are fresh, alert and adequately rested before writing the exam. Just before the exam, don't try to study anything that you haven't already studied. Ideally, you should stop studying at least thirty minutes before the exam.
5. Avoid talking to other students. During exams, most students are anxious and tense. There is no point in their anxiety rubbing off on you.
6. Be careful that you are carrying (and not losing en route) your hall ticket, ID card, spectacles, medications, your trusted writing and drawing instruments, drinking water, calculator (if permitted) and backups. Please do not carry forbidden articles into the exam hall. The last thing you need is to be thrown out.
7. Ensure that you are going to the right centre, at the right date and in time. It's always a good idea to check out the exam centre in advance and familiarize yourself with the right room number and rest room location, especially if you are going there for the first time. Ensure that you leave for the exam centre well in time, thus avoiding tension

during the journey, possible delays due to traffic, weather conditions and traffic jams.
8. Wear comfortable clothes, underclothes and footwear. Your concentration can be completely killed by a pinching shoe or irritating fabric.
9. Do not overeat before the paper. Neither should you go hungry. Use the rest room before you enter the examination hall. If you need a drink of water, do so before the paper, but do not overdo it. A bursting bladder is not a good idea for concentration and focus.
10. Once inside the exam hall well in time, get comfortable, meditate or do deep breathing for a minute or two to calm your mind and repeat the mantra that you will do well in this exam.
11. Do not be in a tearing rush to start answering questions. Take a couple of deep breaths, say a small prayer if need be and then scan the paper to decide which questions you will attempt and in what order (as well as the time you need for each). If you have prepared with mock tests and worked out earlier exam papers with the same time limit, you will be better at this (and less nervous). It's a good idea to keep aside some buffer time for checking your answers. Read all instructions carefully and listen to the examiner. Remember to allocate more time to questions that carry more marks.
12. You do not need to answer the questions in the order that they are presented. It's always a good

idea to first tackle the questions for which you are confident of knowing the material really well. Another good strategy is to answer the shorter questions first so that those marks are guaranteed.
13. Keep a separate rough sheet for scribbles or back-of-the-envelope calculations. If you 'crammed' a large amount of information and are concerned that you may forget, make quick notes of key points on the rough sheet so you can refer to it during the test.
14. Write the correct roll number on the answer sheet (trust me, I have seen students messing this up) and draw margins on the answer sheets so that there is space for the professor to award you marks. Also ensure that the question number you write in the answer sheet matches the question you are actually answering.
15. Avoid smudged writing, general untidiness, overwriting or using ink colours and highlighters that may not be permitted.
16. Even though you may attempt the questions in any order, they must appear in the same order by proper bunching of loose sheets. Scrupulously number your additional sheets and place them in the right order. (This becomes crucial if an answer continues from one loose sheet to the next.) Check once again before tying all the answer sheets securely and submitting your paper.
17. Avoid leaving too much white space between answers. Score out such spaces neatly towards the

end of the exam time, so as to avoid confusing the examiner.
18. After completing the paper, take a deep breath and revise it thoroughly. First check your roll number, then if you have attempted and completed all questions or not. Next complete any unfinished answers. Finally read your answers, correct where needed and add cosmetic changes. If you still have time, repeat the last step.
19. Always write the final conclusion or answer clearly and boldly at the end, preferably underlined. (*Sad story: I got 199 out of 200 in my High School Maths paper because I neglected to write 'Q.E.D.' at the end of a theorem! I understand the current trend is to write 'Thus proved' instead of 'Q.E.D.'*)
20. Avoid spelling mistakes and wrong sentence construction.
21. Always start your answer by stating what you are going to state or prove. (So the teacher is clear that you have understood the question.)
22. With multiple choice answers, cross out the obviously wrong answers immediately. The less choices that remain make it easier to zoom in on the right option.
23. Don't use shortcuts or different methods during exams, especially for maths. Approach the question and follow all the steps as taught in class. Why? Because even if your final answer is wrong, right steps will fetch some marks and wrong steps create distrust even if you have found the right answer.

(Remember though, that you are welcome to use other methods such as Vedic maths, mental arithmetic, etc. in your rough sheets to verify that your answer is correct.)

24. Ensure neat and legible handwriting using a good pen of approved colour, underlining, bullet points and numbered lists, introduction-body-conclusion for essay-type questions and steps for maths questions.

25. Never ever forget to underline the final answer in maths problems, write Q.E.D. at the end of theorems, conclusion at the end of essay questions, a full line at the end of each answer, draw neat and labelled diagrams, flow charts, maps and graphs where needed. They will also fetch you marks even if your final answer is wrong.

26. Attempt only the correct number of questions in each section without wasting time by attempting more questions. If you do not know the answer for a question you planned to attempt, don't waste time pondering over it. Go to the next question and come back to the unfinished sections if time permits.

27. If you must make corrections (also while revising your paper), ensure the corrections are neat and readable without effort. Scoring out the wrong section and writing the revised version is far better than overwriting, or drawing arrows to connect distant sections.

28. Ignore what others are doing or what questions they are tackling. Your entire focus should be on your work.
29. All rough work should be on a separate sheet and clearly marked as such. In addition, if you get ideas about some questions while attempting to answer some other question, jot down those ideas on the sheet kept for rough work. This stops those ideas from distracting you and will serve as reminders when you are attempting those questions.
30. Don't be in a hurry to leave the examination if you finish earlier than expected. Use the bonus time to check, recheck and double-check every answer as well as the neatness of your presentation.
31. Put yourself in the place of the teacher who is correcting your answer sheets. He or she has to correct possibly a hundred answer sheets in a day and that is in addition to usual duties. It is vital that your answer paper should be neatly written, with margins, right question numbers and clear demarcations between answers.
32. In instances where exam papers are handed back to you after being marked, ensure that you review what you got wrong. This should become your focus so that the same mistakes are not repeated.

I am confident that if any student prepares for his or her exam using the recommendations in this book and then follows these guidelines for writing a better exam paper, there is simply no way that he or she cannot get good marks.

Before we conclude …

Before your exams, make sure that you have attempted enough model test papers so that you are confident on the day of your exam. Run through the points we have suggested for handling exams and hit that sixer!

STEP 13: GOING BEYOND MARKS

Mark Twain famously said, 'I've never let my school interfere with my education.' It sounds crazy, but Mark Twain had a point. It is easy to get caught up in the quest for academic excellence and forget that the quest is actually for education as a means to a happy and useful life. There was a time when the goal was education and marks were a by-product. This has been reversed in our education system where marks are the goal and education, the by-product. This is unfortunate.

Let's get a little philosophical here. It is important to accept imperfections in yourself and in others, to keep your ambitions realistic, and to count your blessings. Becoming over-competitive or expecting too much from yourself, your children or your students can be counter-productive. Just observe the high suicide rates in some cram schools in China and in the IIT entrance exams coaching centres in Kota. Not everyone can score a perfect 100, or have a perfect Mensa score of 162, or get gold medals in the Olympics. Try to do better, try to do your best, but maintain your peace of mind, and mental and physical health under all circumstances.

Ever heard of the term *Wabi-sabi*? Wabi-sabi represents a comprehensive Japanese world view or aesthetic based on accepting and embracing transience and imperfection. This concept, derived from the Buddhist teaching of the three marks of existence (impermanence, suffering and emptiness) states that beauty can be 'imperfect, impermanent, and incomplete'. Characteristics of the wabi-sabi aesthetic include elements such as asymmetry, asperity, roughness, irregularity, simplicity, economy and austerity.

So you are probably wondering, 'What do good marks have to do with Wabi-sabi?' Well, the truth is that not everybody can be the class topper or class president. Do try your best, but do not overstrain yourself in scholastic achievements at the cost of physical and mental health. Choose your higher education stream and make your career choice based on your strengths and likings. Then try your best to be outstanding in your career. A competent wall painter can be happier and more successful than an incompetent and disinterested interior designer. Bill Gates, the founder of Microsoft, rightly observed, 'Don't compare yourself with anyone in this world … if you do so, you are insulting yourself.'

There is an Indian legend of a man who carried water from the well to his fields every day, using two large pitchers tied to the ends of a wooden yoke which he placed across his shoulders. The older pitcher had some small cracks, so it was only half full every day by the time the man arrived home. The other pitcher, which was undamaged, was full at the end of each journey, and made fun of the cracked pitcher.

Feeling sorry for its poor performance, the cracked pitcher finally spoke to the man, apologizing for its less-than-satisfactory performance. The man smiled and replied, 'When we return, please observe the path we are using.'

The pitcher now noticed that many flowers and plants were abundantly growing along one side of the path, the side which was being watered daily by its cracks. The man explained, 'Observe the beautiful and abundant plants on your side of the path. I knew about your cracks, and decided to take advantage of them, rather than throwing you away. The water oozing from your cracks has nourished the different flowers, vegetables and fruits growing there.'

Imperfection can be better than perfection at times, and what one feels is a weakness can become a strength if properly utilized. Stop comparing yourself to anyone else.

John Lennon, the extraordinary musician and member of the Beatles, said, 'When I was five years old, my mother always told me that happiness was the key to life. When I went to school, they asked me what I wanted to be when I grew up. I wrote down 'happy'.

'They told me I didn't understand the assignment, and I told them they didn't understand life.'

Please think about it.

THE FOURTEENTH

For those of you who have read *13 Steps to Bloody Good Luck* or *13 Steps to Bloody Good Wealth*, you will recall that we have a particular habit in this particular series: To add a bonus chapter at the end. The bonus chapter is a sweetener. A little reward for having taken out the time to review all thirteen steps in the book.

What we've done for you is rather amazing. We've taken all the material that we presented to you in the thirteen steps of this book and have converted that material into a mind map (remember Step 6: Boost Your Memory?)

Having read this book, all that you now need to do is to review the mind map from time to time. It will help you recall the key deliverables of this book and make you that much more effective in your studying.

REFERENCES
(Also, possible further reading)

1. *13 Steps to Bloody Good Luck* by Ashwin Sanghi
2. *14 Days to Exam Success* by Lucinda Becker
3. *251 Study Secrets* by B. K. Narayan and Preeti Narayan
4. *Brainstorm: The Power and Purpose of the Teenage Brain* by Daniel J. Siegel M.D.
5. *How to Achieve 100% in a GCSE – Guide to GCSE Exam and Revision Technique* by Robert Blakey
6. *How to Become a Straight-A Student: The Unconventional Strategies Real College Students Use to Score High While Studying Less* by Cal Newport
7. *How to Get a First: Insights and Advice from a First-class Graduate* by Michael Tefula
8. *I Hate Revision: Study Skills and Revision Techniques for GCSE, A-level and Undergraduate Exams* by Robert Blakey
9. *Ignited Minds* by Dr. A. P. J. Abdul Kalam
10. *Ready, Study, Go!* by Khurshed Batliwala and Dinesh Gokhale
11. *Six Secrets Smart Students Don't Tell You* by Chandan Deshmukh
12. *Speed Reading: How to Double (or Triple) Your Reading Speed and Become an Effective Learner* by Oliver Thompson
13. *Study Skills Essentials: Oxford Graduates Reveal Their Study Tactics, Essay Secrets and Exam Advice* by Patrick McMurray
14. *Study Smarter, Not Harder* by Kevin Paul
15. *Super Brain: Unleashing the Explosive Power of Your Mind to Maximize Health, Happiness, and Spiritual Well-Being* by Rudolph E. Tanzi and Deepak Chopra
16. *The Art of Study* by Dr. Vijay Agrawal
17. *The Memory Book* by Harry Lorayne and Jerry Lucas
18. *The Power of Focus* by Jack Canfield and others
19. *The Study Skills Book* by Dr. Kathleen McMillan
20. *The Study Skills Handbook* by Stella Cottrell
21. *Use Your Head* by Tony Buzan
22. *What Smart Students Know: Maximum Grades. Optimum Learning. Minimum Time* by Adam Robinson
23. *Word Up!* by Marcia Riefer Johnston

www.ingramcontent.com/pod-product-compliance
Lightning Source LLC
LaVergne TN
LVHW010330070526
838199LV00065B/5712